ALSO BY
Paul Durcan

Endsville
(with Brian Lynch)
O Westport in the Light of Asia Minor
Teresa's Bar
Sam's Cross
Jesus, Break His Fall
The Ark of the North
The Selected Paul Durcan
(edited by Edna Longley)
Jumping the Train Tracks with Angela
The Berlin Wall Café
Going Home to Russia
In the Land of Punt
(with Gene Lambert)
Jesus and Angela
Daddy, Daddy
Crazy About Women
A Snail in My Prime: New and Selected Poems
Give Me Your Hand
Christmas Day
Greetings to Our Friends in Brazil
Cries of an Irish Caveman
Paul Durcan's Diary
The Art of Life
The Laughter of Mothers
Life is a Dream: 40 Years Reading Poems 1967–2007
Praise in Which I Live and Move and Have My Being

THE DAYS OF SURPRISE

Paul Durcan

The Days of Surprise

Harvill *Secker*
LONDON

Published by Harvill Secker 2015

2 4 6 8 10 9 7 5 3

First published in Great Britain in 2015 by
HARVILL SECKER
Random House
20 Vauxhall Bridge Road
London SW1V 2SA

www.vintage-books.co.uk

A Penguin Random House Company

Penguin
Random House
UK

global.penguinrandomhouse.com

A CIP catalogue record for this book is available from the British Library

ISBN 9781846559716 (hardback)

The Penguin Random House Group Limited supports the Forest Stewardship
Council® (FSC®), the leading international forest-certification organisation. Our
books carrying the FSC label are printed on FSC®-certified paper. FSC is the only
forest-certification scheme supported by the leading environmental organisations,
including Greenpeace. Our paper procurement policy can be found at
www.randomhouse.co.uk/environment

MIX
Paper from
responsible sources
FSC® C016897

Typeset in Bembo by Palimpsest Book Production Limited,
Falkirk, Stirlingshire

Printed and bound in Great Britain by Clays Ltd, St Ives plc

To David Rieff
Walking Up and Down the Earth

Acknowledgements

To Aosdána and to the Arts Council of the Republic of Ireland.

To John McHugh of the Achill Heinrich Böll Association and the Westport Custom House Studios.

To Dr Cliona Ni Riordain, Paul Bensimon, Carla Daly, Mary MacBride Walsh, Harriet Waugh, Richard Dorment, Niall MacMonagle, Dermot Bolger, Deirdre Madden, Dorrie Darlington, Margaret McLoughlin, Brent Parker, Sheila Sullivan, Father Patrick O'Brien, Harry Clifton, Eimer Philbin Bowman, Brendan Flynn, Brian Fallon, the late Sally McGuire, Eileen O'Mara Walsh, Caitríona O'Reilly, Bill Swainson, Brian Lynch, Conor O'Callaghan, Catriona Crowe, Cormac Kinsella and Peter Straus.

To Padraic, Lorraine and Patrick Carr.

Very special thanks to Declan Heeney of Gill Hess and to Elizabeth Foley and Fiona Murphy of Harvill Secker and to Ian Pindar.

Versions of five of these poems were published in *Poetry Salzburg Review* No. 25, the *Irish Times* and in the *Irish University Review* Seamus Heaney special issue. 'Portrait of the Painter' was a filmed document in 'The Edward McGuire Studio Contents' collaboration in March 2014 between the Irish Museum of Modern Art and the Institute of Art, Design and Technology, Dún Laoghaire.

Contents

On these the iniquity of oblivion hath blindly scattered her poppy.

Helen Waddell, *The Wandering Scholars*
(London, 1927)

THE DAYS OF SURPRISE

57 Dartmouth Square

I was three years of age in the full of my days,
Never again to be so fully myself.
I was my home, my home was my name –
57 Dartmouth Square.
All that I was, now and for ever,
Today, yesterday and tomorrow,
57 Dartmouth Square.
Sometimes I was called Paul
But mostly I was not a who or a what
But a where.

I was a place.
In the sixty-odd years that were to follow
(Which fortunately I had no foreknowledge of)
I would never again know such apotheosis
As the place that I was, 1947–48.
I answered to the name of Paul, to that fearful call –
'Paul! Paul!' –
But knowing that my real name,
My identity tag stitched in red thread
On white cotton on my grey socks,
Was 57 Dartmouth Square.
Heaven was a place – not a placeless heaven –
And I was that place –
57 Dartmouth Square.

57 Dartmouth Square
Was a Victorian terrace house
On the Grand Canal in Dublin
Between Charlemont Street Bridge and Leeson
    Street Bridge
Built for British Army officers
And their families in the late 1890s.

1947–48 there was myself and my mother,
My father gone away for a long time
To stand in County Mayo in the general election
On the Clann na Poblachta ticket. With the ticket
He'd come home at weekends, presenting me with
    the ticket
To play with – roll upon roll of election tickets.

1947–48 when I walked in and out of myself,
57 Dartmouth Square,
Holding hands with Mummy,
I was a three-storey, red-brick terraced house
With two flights of granite steps to a hall door
With a recessed porch
In which I never dallied, not even to play in.
I entered only the basement to come in and out of
    myself,
The same as the coalman humping
Sacks of coal and slack on his bent shoulders,
The same as the newspaper man,

All twenty-one stone of him,
His tar-black streaky hair drenched in hair oil,
His yellow lined face more ancient than parchment.

Holding hands with Mummy on winter mornings
We'd walk along the Square, its high black palings,
Under house-high sycamores and limes,
To the far side of it where the Grand Canal,
High up in its road, flowed
From Charlemont Street Bridge to Leeson Street
    Bridge.

We'd climb up wide steps, Mummy and I,
And stand on the towpath to watch the barge
Inside the lock gates rising up
Like Jesus in the Resurrection story
Until the barge achieved its glory and began to chug
Between the banks, its cargo under tarpaulin,
A man in a cloth cap at the tiller, smoking a
    cigarette,
A man's bicycle thrown down at his feet on the
    deck,
All handlebars, crossbar, raw naked leather saddle.

Much as I enjoyed being 57 Dartmouth Square,
My name, role and function as 57 Dartmouth
    Square,
One day I'd cease to be 57 Dartmouth Square,

Becoming instead the *Barge Man at the Tiller*
In a Cloth Cap, smoking a cigarette.
It was my fate to be a happy neurotic.
In the winter of 1947–48 holding Mummy's hand,
Knowing where I was, I'd reached already the
    Promised Land,
The remainder of my life I would spend
Waiting for the Three Wise Men to find me.

6 May 1954 Dr Roger Bannister broke the four-
    minute mile
At the Iffley Road Track in Oxford
And being a skinlessly searching nine-year-old
    boy-child
I wanted also to break the four-minute mile.
Four laps of Dartmouth Square on the footpath
Constituted approximately the magic mile.
I went into training, racing around the Square
With the boy next door, John Richardson,
Hurtling around its corners, tut-tutting pedestrians
Stepping aside to pre-empt catastrophic collisions.

The Square was padlocked and in winter
The girls of the Loreto Convent, St Stephen's Green,
Played hockey in it, a pre-Christian field game
From the era when a human being carried a club
    and a stone.
In my bedroom window I sat repining

And aching at their stickwork – flicking, pushing,
    scooping –
In their long tomato-red skirts, white shirts and ties.
Bully! Bully! Bully! Bully! Bully!
Pubescence is a beastly process.

In the summertime youths from The Hill on Mount
    Pleasant
Climbed over the high black palings to play soccer –
Only to be chased and beaten out of it by the
    Garda Síochána,
A respectable resident having telephoned a
    complaint:
A shocking epiphany of my child's accumulating
    horror
At the cracks – no, the chasms – in the social fabric
    of Dublin.

Christmas Day was not really Christmas Day,
It was the day of Santa Claus, an eccentric deity
Whom my father's corpulent pal, Judge Charlie
    Conroy,
Pointed out to me one night catwalking the
    rooftops.
The real Christmas Day was the Feast of the
    Epiphany, 6 January,
When at long and dear last in the suspenseful chess
    game of life

I got to move the Three Wise Men into the Crib.
At last they had found me and I wriggled in ecstasy.
How ecstatic also seemed these three exotic
    refugees,
Melchior, Caspar and Balthasar.
Hailing from the farthest corners of the universe,
From China, Lithuania, Ethiopia.
On the Feast of the Epiphany
In the hallway of 57 Dartmouth Square
Into the Crib on the hall table
I moved the Three Wise Men into position,
A stick of liquorice dangling from my mouth.
I had become again the happy neurotic I aspired
    to be.

Other Boys' Mothers

Between the ages of ten and twelve
I could not keep myself out of the beds
Of the young mothers of my schoolmates.
What with homework, football, cricket, athletics,
Life was hectic-complicated in the years 1954 to 1956:
From the four-minute mile to the Hungarian Uprising.
Yet for all its hectic-complications and heart-renderings
I would not have had it any other way:
Those years of the savouring of the respectable breasts –
Of the wine-tasting of the exclusive bosom-yards –
O of all those scented, sandy, salty, sea-weedy undulations
Of the grinning, gleeful, omnipotent young mothers
   of my schoolmates.

First Mixed Party

In 1959, aged fifteen, I was invited to a mixed party –
A MIXED party! –
In the house of Mr and Mrs Thomas Doyle, S.C.
In Winton Road off the Appian Way
By printed invitation,
Black italics on gilt-edged white card.
After a council of war my parents gave me permission,
My father ruling against it, but my mother overruling
    him;
The MIXTURE being surprisingly of boys and girls,
Caterpillars and tigers, corncrakes and polar bears.
Up till then I had only ever been at orgies for little boys
At which we beat each other up with pillows and
    cushions,
Doing our damnedest to wreck our parents' homes.

To the gramophone accompaniment of Buddy Holly
    super-stuttering
'Peggy Sue' and 'Rave On',
Elvis Presley – 'incarnate evil' our Jesuit maths teacher
    had confided in us –
Honking huskily on a leash 'Hound Dog'
Or shivering catatonically in his 'Blue Suede Shoes'
Or oiling his adenoids with 'Wooden Heart',
Jerry Lee Lewis going off his rocker,
Boys and girls circled around each other,

Animals not of different species but from different
    planets.
I gawked at clusters of teenage females
As if they were flocks of ostriches
Which they were – except
For the two or three orang-outangs among them
Whom we pimply puritanical prigs
Knowingly dismissed as 'flirts' –
Not knowing what the word 'flirt' meant – exactly.

I, of course, immediately fell in love with Fiona,
Being a lifelong mortally wounded Romantic
Since the age of four and a half.
I had my first love affair at seven
With Andrea who had freckles and red hair –
She walked to school on the other side of the road,
Eyed by me already in the viral clutches of Venus;
I dumped her for Jacqueline, who also had freckles and
    red hair,
Because Jacqueline sat on the grass with me making
    daisy chains.

After three hours of agonised eyeballing
And the central light had been switched off
Leaving only one standard lamp and two table lamps,
When we thought nobody was looking
We exchanged telephone numbers, Fiona and I.
The next day when I came home from school
In the blackening gloom of a late North European
    afternoon,

My mother in the cold dark kitchen to which she had
    been consigned in perpetuity,
Sighing, stammered: 'Your father wants to speak to you
    in The Study.'

My father had a room of his own
Which he called The Study.
He stood up from behind his desk
And grimaced at me with incredulity:
'Do you know what you have done?'
Quivering – I knew where this dialogue was going to
    conclude –
I replied truthfully 'No'.
He continued – waving his right arm in the air
Like Robespierre addressing the Estates-General
(My father was a devotee of Robespierre) –
'Do you know from whom I have received a
    telephone call?'
'N – n – no' I replied, barely able to stutter.
'Mrs Mona O'Connor – one of the most respectable
Ladies in the whole of the island of Ireland –
Mrs Mona O'Connor of Roscommon.
Do you know what she told me?
Mrs Mona O'Connor of Roscommon informed me
That at that social whatever-it-was last night,
Which in the first place you never should have
    attended,
You were observed – observed! – wearing a – a – a –
    a BLACK shirt!'
Whereupon instead of unbuckling his trousers belt

With which to give me an unmerciful thrashing,
Which would be his normal course of action,
He slumped back down into his swivel chair, groaning:
'A black shirt!
Are you cognisant of what you have done?
A black shirt!
Where did you come from? Who are you?
Will I always have to be ashamed of you for the rest
of my days?
Mrs Mona O'Connor of Roscommon, *what* will she
think of us?'

The Actors' Chapel,
239 West 49th Street

for Belinda McKeon

I

October 1960, JFK about to be elected president,
Putting Richard Milhous Nixon to the sword on TV,
Enter our new English teacher and games-master
   Mr Kelly, S.J.
From Tullamore, County Offaly,
In his mid-twenties, halfway through his Jesuit novitiate –
'A Scholastic', the Society of Jesus dub him –
Handsomer than any man we have ever set eyes on,
Twenty-five of us fifteen-year-old boys
In our fourth year of secondary school
At a new, small, Jesuit day school in Dublin,
More glamorous than Marlon Brando and John F.
   Kennedy synthesised,
His ice-white teeth, his suntanned, wind-blown face,
His jet-black hair parted, plastered in Brylcreem,
His white Roman collar so steep
You would think he had the neck of a racehorse,
A thoroughbred filly,
His black soutane sprouting wings at his shoulder blades,
Black wings which streamed behind him as he strode
   out
Across the lawn from the priests' house
To the school house for first class at 9 a.m.

A few of us instantaneously got a crush on Mr Kelly,
  S.J.
An all-or-nothing crush
With all that ecstasy and all that misery that an all-or-
    nothing crush foments.
All our hormones magnifying the Lord;
Whether it was in the classroom or on the rugby field
We were the chosen few who would die for Mr Kelly
And in the long nights of sleepless loneliness
And unrequited passion
And the sky-high spumante of the creamiest fountains
I agonised if Mr Kelly felt the same way about me
As I felt about him – that beseeching, that yearning,
That pining to possess or be possessed
By a man's man, who was also as feminine
As any matinée idol of the silver screen –
Marilyn Monroe or Audrey Hepburn.
There was no way of knowing his inner feelings for us,
Other than flares and flashes
Of his instinctive good nature,
His seriousness, his laughter, his sense of fun,
His code of truth-telling and manliness,
His athletic prowess, his fierce anger
At any manifestation of meanness or injustice by one of
    his boys –
His young soldiers on the field of play.

Once when in mid-winter at wing-forward in a
    line-out
I indulged in a wanton shoulder-charge, he gave me

A blast of his whistle, a penalty to the opposition and a
    warning
That the next time he would send me back to the
    dressing room.
The disappointment on his face as well as the anger
Made me want to evaporate on the spot.
Yet a week later when from a scrum
Near our opponents' goal-line – Blackrock College
    (Holy Ghosts) –
As a blind-side wing-forward I nipped in for a try
His approval was so filled with delight
That it became a flying carpet
On which I flew home to my mother and father
Across the rooftops of the inner suburbs of Dublin –
Ranelagh and Leeson.

In class he taught us Gerard Manley Hopkins
Or, to try and tell the truth, he read with us Gerard
    Manley Hopkins
With such gentleness, quietude, piety, ardour,
    bewilderment
'The Wreck of the Deutschland'.
Without comprehending it we knew that Hopkins also
Was up there beyond the stars, beyond Elvis
And Marlon and Jimmy and Orson,
Elizabeth Taylor and Sophia Loren
And Bobby Charlton and Duncan Edwards
And Roger Bannister and Emil Zatopek
And Tony O'Reilly and Ulick O'Connor
And Jack Kyle and Ronnie Delany

And Johnny Caldwell and Freddie Gilroy
And Rocky Marciano and Dick McTaggart.
Only Cassius Clay came near to Hopkins.

II

This morning – fifty-four years later –
On West 49th Street between Broadway and Eighth –
In the Actors' Chapel
I ask a young middle-aged priest if I might meet Fr Joe
    Kelly, S.J.
Whom, a long time ago, I had heard, worked here.
'Fr Kelly passed away three years ago,' he answered
    without feeling.
If anything slightly coldly, I thought – a shocking
    thought.
'Damn your soul!' I said to him speechlessly. 'Damn
    your soul!'

'You are one of many people
Who come here asking for him.'

At the back of the Actors' Chapel
I stood before the icon
Of a tall, striking, young man in a red gown in a blue
    sky,
Under which I read the words:
St Genesius. Actor. Martyr.
The serrated tears of reality crawled down my face:
The vision of a young man from Tullamore, County
    Offaly

In a small day school in Dublin in the late 1950s, early
    1960s,
Inspiring young boys to believe in poetry, revolution
    and justice —
To have faith in play —
Who in the second half of his life as a Jesuit priest
In a Chapel on Broadway helped actors to keep the faith,
Who, when the rats of stage fright
Came scuttling across the actors' feet,
Stood in the wings with the Vomit Bucket
Healing them when they needed healing,
Just as they healed him
When he was in need of healing himself
In the Sahara hours of 3 p.m. in the afternoon
Or 3 a.m. in the middle of the night.
Mr Kelly, S.J., have mercy on me.
Mr Kelly, S.J., pray for me.
Ave Maria, gratia plena, Dominus tecum,
Benedicta tu in mulieribus
Et benedictus fructus ventris tui, Jesus.

III

The door of our chapel
Is always open on to the public street,
So that when at the Consecration
I kneel to genuflect,
As I climb to my feet
To elevate the Host
I can see across West 49th Street
The name over the steps:

THE MAYFAIR HOTEL.
God only knows
Who you might see
Going in or out
As you elevate the Host
Or the Chalice,
Coming down the steps
Or going up the steps
Of THE MAYFAIR HOTEL.
Between genuflection
And elevation
In that gold hole of a moment
I have seen
In a glimpse
Sinéad Cusack,
Donal McCann,
Dearbhla Molloy,
Dermot Crowley,
Maggie Smith,
Lambert Wilson,
Woody Allen,
Ingrid Craigie,
Donal O'Kelly,
Marie Mullen,
Seán McGinley,
Colm Tóibín,
Sam Shepard,
Jessica Lange,
Simon Callow –
Their shorn-off

Gleaming faces
Particles of the Host,
Droplets of blood,
Sweat and tears
Of particular people
In New York City.
Go now in peace
To love and serve the Lord,
The Mass is ended.
I cover you all with my wings,
Exit into sacristy darkness,
Leaving the great doors open
Onto West 49th Street and Eighth:
The Actors' Chapel.

The Poet and the Judge

My father was known as 'The Judge'
For the not unjust reason
That he worked as a judge –
A judge of the assize –
The Judge on the Western Circuit of Ireland,
The counties of Mayo and Galway:
Silence in court – the Judge is coming in!
Cried the Crier John Freyne from under the Reporters'
    Gallery.

On a winter's night in Dublin
After spending four or five hours in Dwyer's public
    house
In Lower Leeson Street quaffing pints –
Pints of Phoenix –
I suggested to the poet Mike Hartnett
That we purchase a half-dozen bottles of Phoenix
And repair to my parents' home in 57 Dartmouth Square
Up the street and over the canal bridge
And listen to my LPs of Buddy and Elvis and Fats
And Lightnin' and Sonny and John Lee
And Little Richard and Ray Charles and Jerry Lee
    Lewis – the Rocket.
My parents would be long gone to bed
At the top of the Victorian, three-storey, red-brick
    terrace house.

Settling in nicely in the downstairs basement breakfast
    room
Mike took a mahogany dining chair and, laying it on
    its back,
Lay down on the carpet, put his feet up
And, lighting up a fag – a Woodbine – gave me a drag.
To make ourselves comfortable was the thing.
(Five years later we'd have been rolling joints.)
I sat in an armchair, pleased that the poet, my
    prodigious friend,
Had made himself so immediately at home.

Hours seemed to pass, such was our mystical
    contentment
Puffing smoke rings, imbibing, listening,
So that when the door opened as if of its own accord
This seemed a natural happening as well as
    synchronicity
Until in the doorway we saw
The 100 per cent embodiment of my father the Judge
In navy-blue dressing gown with red cord, yellow
    tassels.
He peered down at Mike, and Mike peered back up at
    the Judge,
Blowing him, it seemed, an extra smoke ring
As a signal of mutual esteem and recognition.
'Mr Hartnett!' my father declaimed.
'Do you not think you should be at home in your
    own bed?'

'If you say so, Judge, if you say so.'
'I do say so, Mr Hartnett, I do say so.'
Mike, charming to the last cannon ball exploding
    on the field of a lost battle in Austria, cried out:
'*Oíche mhaith, a Bhreitheamh Uasal!*'
(Goodnight to Thee, O Noble Judge!)

First we tittered, a pair of truant, precocious schoolgirls;
Then we split our sides laughing
Until we subsided in shocked silence.
'Christ!' muttered Mike. 'I had better make tracks.'
I let him out the side door into the spear-carrying
    night
Of Dartmouth Square, palinged and padlocked:
Thirty years later, while I myself was moaning and
    groaning and pining away
Alone in a cave in the Docklands,
Mike was to make his home with kind Angela Liston
In the Dartmouth Square of the Judge, the padlocks
    and the high black palings.

Youth

after Veronica Bolay

Who can communicate the grief of youth?
There I was in 1963 alone in my bedroom
Hour after hour at the window
In the month of June watching the rain
Falling slant with no hope or mercy.
'Have you ever seen me pissing?'
I hear a man asking a passer-by on the street . . .

Our neighbour Mr Foster, the wealthy proprietor
Of a neon sign company.
At five o'clock in the afternoon
A taxi brings him home every day
And whether or not there is an actual passer-by
He cries out the crucial, historical question:
'Have you ever seen me pissing?'
Before proceeding to urinate through his own railings.

Unable to speak to my parents, to anyone,
Pining for a *Fräulein* with yellow hair
Who, when I first walked out with her,
Laughed with abandon in derision
That I believed the colour
Of her hair was really yellow.

'Don't you know yet?' she cried.
'Oh, Paul, you are so naive!
You are such a child it's not true!'

But of course it is she
Who is the purest fool,
Not knowing even my real name:
I, Kierkegaard, Nietzsche, Van Gogh,
Bent over on my upright chair
With either my head in my hands
Or my hand across my face,
My legs crossed,
My black boots, my blue velvet jacket.

If I take my own life
She will mock me.
Yet only by taking my own life
Can I demonstrate to her
With all the gay genius of me
The grief of youth.
In my bedroom with fissured gold wallpaper
My big pink painting on its easel is blank.

Il Bambino Dormiente

Last Tuesday I nipped over to Venice for a day and a
    night:
I needed to see one particular painting in the
    Gallerie dell'Accademia
By Giovanni Bellini:
The Madonna Enthroned Adoring the Sleeping Child –
Il Bambino Dormiente.
Needed to? Yes – needed to.
On the spit of dissolution,
Estranged from my family,
I needed to see again
The most affectionate yet sacred family portrait ever
    painted.
Cheap Aer Lingus flight to Marco Polo,
Bus into the bus station in the Piazzale Roma,
Water bus down the Grand Canal to the Gallerie
    dell'Accademia,
Half-price entrance fee for a European pensioner.

Not many visitors. In a vast stone hall
I linger alone before Bellini's small picture
Of all that it means to be your mother's son
In the mortal world, all that it means
To be a young mother doomed. I needed –
As we need to drink water to stave off death –
I needed to see myself as originally I was:

A naked male infant draped naked across my
    mother's knees,
Sleeping the sleep of death;
I needed to see her slightly prised-open eyes
    glancing down
At his sleeping visage, his tall, thin, grey, aged
    features –
Il Bambino Dormiente.
I needed to see again with my own eyes
Her apprehension of the inevitable;
To check again that she does indeed have red hair
Parted down the middle
In a white veil
Under the flat gold plate of her halo
And that her cheeks also are red –
Not with rouge –
But with all
That is most virginal, auroral,
Most purely West of Ireland peasant princess,
Palestinian Jewess,
Her slender fingers craned tall in prayer.
I linger – I linger all day.

I stayed overnight in a nearby *pensione*
On the Rio di San Trovaso,
'The Villa of Miracles', which between the two
    world wars
Was the Soviet Russian Embassy.
(The concierge archly confided in me:
'We still receive the Russian clients.')

In the middle of the night, after a catnap,
Having churned back up the waters of the Grand
    Canal,
To the bus station in the Piazzale Roma –
A young Chinese woman named Ya
From Yunnan Province studying in Manchester
HUMAN RESOURCES
Helping me find the bus to Treviso –
I got a Ryanair early flight back to Dublin
To settle my affairs and get ready for my own little
    sleep,
Meeting my mother in the big deep.

Meeting Mother in the Big O

In the room the women come and go
Most certainly not talking of Michelangelo.
One among them, though,
Stays faithful to the end. No
Matter how bad things go,
Mother will meet me, and so

This early, sunny morning after the big solo
Party I threw last night in the col-
D, cold alcoves of the East Link Toll
Bridge in camera we meet in the Big O –
She wants 'to pluck with me a crow' –
'Show me it,' she crows, 'your big toe.'

She does not scold me for putting my big toe
In it – 'What right,' she cries, 'have they to say No
When a Little Boy at the end of his Mayo
Requires to go? So?
So what? Only now that it is all o-
Ver, rejoice in your new life in the Big O!'

And a sword shall pierce through your own soul.

A Fitting Epitaph

'He's a bit lacking in the Upstairs Department'
Is what my mother, smiling proudly,
Used to say of me,
Especially to Mr Joseph McGovern
Of McGoverns of Camden Street, drapers,
When she was in the act of purchasing for me
A pair of short trousers –
'He's a bit lacking in the Upstairs Department' –
An image somehow that explained everything
That needed to be explained about her firstborn –
At which Mr Joseph McGovern
Would cast his eyes up to heaven –
i.e., the ceiling –
And looking down at me smile a slightly sickly smile:
'He's a bit lacking in the Upstairs Department':
A fitting epitaph.

A Charm of Goldfinches

The pair of us were sitting alone in the empty public
    house –
The door wide open to the city street – on a summer's
    morning,
Drinking two quiet pints, myself and Justin.
Justin ventured a single rhetorical question:
'Did you ever set eyes on a charm of goldfinches?'
High up in the corner of the ceiling
Hung a cage with a goldfinch:
A scarlet-faced bird with a yellow bar on its wing
    feather
And a black-and-white chequered rump and tail.
Without uttering, we ordered two more pints
And the barman skedaddled back out again into the
    lounge.
Justin put two fingers to his lips and winked at me,
Got to his feet and strode over to the corner,
Stood under the cage and unlatched it.
The goldfinch on its perch peered down
Into Justin's eager, kindly, glittering eyes
And Justin looked back down at me –
And space stations of silence seemed to orbit us,
Which amounted in actuality to maybe thirty seconds
And without a tinkle the goldfinch swooped out of the
    cage
And flew around the bar room,

Diving, circling, darting, weaving, whirling, veering,
    hopping,
Before flying straight out into the street
Never to be seen again – by us.
Justin in his blacker-than-coal, sleek black beard
Under his sleek, thick mane of blacker-than-coal hair
Smiled the most extravagantly other-worldly smile
I had ever seen him smile
And we both folded our arms
Across our breasts
And swallowed, as deeply from enlightenment
As from our pint glasses.
Out on the street he rubbed his hands together with
    gratification.
An Lasair Choille, Mac Duarcáin – cried Justin – *Flame
    of the Woods,*
Son of the Melancholy Man, Thistle-Seed Glutton!
We bid farewell to one another
And until death did us part
Neither of us would ever speak of that summer's
    morning again.

Waiting for Essex Woman

for B. G. McCall

I

Waiting for Essex Woman —
Are you really going to come
Into my night redder than the stars —
Into my green-eyed dawn?

If and when you come
Will you unclasp your golden lunula?
Goldener than all the golden furze
Of the tombs of Sutton Hoo and Tara.

Will we be gentler with one another
Than heretofore it has been thought
Evolutionarily conceivable?
Gentler than lions?

II

And after we have shook hands
And exchanged pennants
I will run a mile or so,
While you are warming up
For your discus throw.

33

In the doorway I peer out at a vista
Of black popes, lines of them,
In the drizzling rain,
Far as the eye can see.
Alleluia!
The hegemony of the white man is over.
If not in sackcloth but in ashes,
I will pray not only for a black pope
But for a black Archbishop of Dublin.
We Irish also have had enough
Of the hegemony of the white Irishman.
What is more, I will pray like a madman
For a black woman Archbishop of Dublin.
I am dust, and unto dust I shall return.

The Days of Surprise

The morning after the election of Francis,
In Ringsend Church at 11.45 a.m.,
Empty except for the smudge of my own presence –
Serious silence. *Silenzio!*
The sole sound is the sound of silence:
Silenzio, which is the chord of the lowly, chosen one,
Jorge Mario Bergoglio of Buenos Aires,
Silenzio, which is the carnival of his soul,
Silenzio, which is the mother and father of effortlessness,
Silenzio, which is the concentration of the child,
Silenzio, which is singing
'I am listening to you';
Silenzio, which is whispering 'Let me embrace you';
Silenzio, which is smiling 'Let me kiss your feet.'

At the altar-rail I gaze
At the noticeboard of the First Holy Communion children,
Each with their unique pledge:
Rosita Mulhall, aged 7:
'I PROMISE TO CLEAN MY ROOM.'
Chloe Swift, aged 8:
'I PROMISE TO PLAY WITH LUKE.'
Lisa Jordan, aged 7:
'I PROMISE TO FOLLOW JESUS
BY HOOVERING FOR MY MAM.'

Outside, around the church, the village swirls
And swarms like the hundreds of brent geese
Jinking overhead and the seagulls swooping
Like in a painting by a child or Mark Joyce
Or Gerard Dillon or Giotto or Fra Angelico
Or Ian Fairweather or Nicolas de Staël or Tony O'Malley.
As the church bell tolls the angelus at noon
The traffic lights conduct the people,
The buildings in the village like in Buenos Aires
All at angles with one another –
All gables, chimney pots, railings –
The barber shop, Tesco Express, HQ Dry Cleaners,
The three public houses – The Yacht, The Oarsman,
    Sally's Return –
The Bridge Café, the pharmacy, Ladbrokes bookmaker's,
The library with its Chinese granite benches,
The health centre, the Master Butcher's,
Ferrari's Takeaway, Spar,
The charity shop, the wine shop, the humpbacked bridge
Under which, behind Ringsend Church, the River
    Dodder flows
Like a little mare over the last fence
At Cheltenham or Punchestown,
Before it breasts the line at the winning post,
Its rider bent over double
Like the Angel at the Annunciation,
And meets the River Liffey and the sea.

The tide is in and Francis has come back
From Assisi to stroll again amongst us,
To announce the affinity of all creatures –

Child, kitten, woman, puppy, man, lamb, foal,
Prisoner, judge, sick, elderly,
Buggy baby, Zimmer-frame lady.
On the ledge between the church gable and the high river,
Alongside the council flats of the working people –
The aristocracy of the poor –
The flood-lit, blue-and-white statue on its Dublin
    granite plinth –
Our Lady, barefoot, smiling upon the waters,
And upon Jorge Mario Bergoglio – Papa Francesco.

Standing up in the back of an open jeep
In the middle of the piazza in his white shop coat,
Instead of the Papal Blessing
He gives us the thumbs-up sign –
'Have a nice Sunday, have a good lunch';
Smiling a good smile,
Again he gives us the thumbs-up sign –
'This is what we do in Argentina –
Be amicable to your neuroses.'

From the hump of the bridge I say to him,
With the greyhound track behind me
And the Sugar Loaf and the Dublin mountains,
Brimming with *silenzio*, Thomas Merton's prayer:
'May the Most Holy Mother of God
Obtain for your soul light and peace and strength
And may her Holy Child
Be your joy and protection at all times.'

14 March 2013

St Peter's Square, Sunday Morning, 27 April 2014

Pleasant, mild, drizzly Sunday morning in spring
In St Peter's Square – the canonisation of John XXIII and
    John Paul II –
Thanks to the loving-kindness of a self-effacing Polish
    seminarian
I find myself one of fifteen or twenty
In a pigeonhole above Bernini's Colonnade
Looking directly down on Papa Francesco in his chair –
    not a throne –
More a kitchen chair than a throne.
On being introduced to a venerable Benedictine monk,
His sadistic superciliousness takes me by surprise.

His cynical arrogance, his omniscient vanity,
His amused misogyny, his bully-boy abuse,
His *sotto voce* dismissal of and ridicule and contempt for
This Sunday morning of carnival, of universal human
    holiness –
His derision of sanctity –
His mockery of Angelo Roncalli and Karol Wojtyła,
His ignorance of both;
His urinal-stall mouth, his stick-it-in-your face paunch,
His eyebrows crawling all over you,
His spilling-over jowls cowled
In all the fatty finery of snobbery,

Wined and dined in high society,
His cold flat eyes devoid of fish –
Caricature of all that St Benedict of Monte Cassino was;
Fifty years spouting the Rule –
Always betraying every word of it;
Power-sated cleric of the twenty-first century
Who has not abandoned God,
Because he has never waited for God in the first place;
Wallowing in his own smugness,
A scandalous, venerable Benedictine monk giving scandal.

In desperation for help and succour and inspiration,
I gaze down at Papa Francesco in his chair,
A figure of childlike passivity
As well as of childlike authority,
Blinking,
His face a study in concentration,
Of all the thoughtfulness of a dreaming child
On the brink of a miraculous breakthrough,
His hands in his lap.
I close my eyes and carry Papa Francesco –
The man of constant surprise –
Back to Ireland with me:
Memories, dreams and reflections
Of Karol Wojtyła and Angelo Roncalli;
Of the Polish orphan poet and the Bergamesque peasant
    peacemaker;
Of their happy neuroses;
Of their 'exquisite openness to the Holy Spirit'.

The Young Mother on the Country Bus in El Salvador

On a country bus in El Salvador
About twenty-eight years ago,
Father Sam found himself seated next
A young Salvadoran mother
Breastfeeding her infant daughter.
Father Sam blurted out:
'*Que hermosa niña!*
What a beautiful baby girl!'
She smiled and when she came
To the end of a passage of breastfeeding
She took Father Sam's right hand
In her own right hand
And placed it across her left breast:
'It is good, Papa,' she smiled, 'it is good.'

Our Lady of Westport
after Patrick Pye

Mary the Mother of Jesus –
The most elegant woman in Westport.
Behold her striding around the foothills of the Reek,
Aughagower, Old Head, Boheh, Drummin, Murrisk –
A sight for sore eyes.
In her bottle-green cowled habit, her white scarf,
Her bare feet,
She hangs out on the corner of the Mall
With her little man in the palm of her hand,
As ebullient a wee covey in his coral-pink judo-strip
As ever kicked a ball for the County of Mayo.
They say she's from Syria or Israel or Lebanon or
    Palestine or
One of them places and that she gave birth to him
In a hay barn on a small farm out beyond Louisburgh
    or some place.
Tell you something for nothing:
That woman would make you want to be human –
Our Lady of Westport.

The Last Great Achill Island Volkswagen Beetle Protestant

I am the last great Achill Island Volkswagen Beetle
    Protestant.
There are few of us,
But we get value for our perseverance:
A spare, simple service
In the King James verse;
The Eucharist
In both species;
And, if it is the rector on the altar,
A sermon of pure poetry –
Presence and peace.

Bury me in Dugort
Under the height
Where the light
Never goes out
And the door is never shut
And, matching the Celtic cross,
A portable loo
Outside the sacristy
Open twenty-four hours, day and night.
In the Dictatorship of the Wind Turbines
A last great Achill Island Volkswagen Beetle
    Protestant

Need never fear of being taken short,
Especially not in the last minutes of his or her life.
The Lord shall preserve thy going out and thy coming in
From this time forth, and even for evermore.

Meeting the Great Consultant

After having fasted from midnight, I get a taxi at noon,
Driven by an easygoing, affable Wexfordman from the
    Hook –
He confesses that he finds modern hospitals 'scary' –
To the Hospital – Level 5, Day Care –
For what the Great Consultant's secretary by phone
Has told me will be 'a procedure'.
As with anything to do with Health, it's a Stations of
    the Cross
The purpose of which is to cause the patient maximum
    humiliation and stress.
Reception: a mean-looking, middle-aged lady with
    dyed blonde hair;
Canine, snub-nosed, dismissive.
Onward to the ward: two young female nurses –
One human and warm and gay and bright and helpful;
The other brittle, curt, bent on making a nuisance of
    herself –
Flings open cubicle curtains, instructs me
To get into a trolley bed.
Having undressed and wrapped up in a surgical
    gown –
The usual, humdrum, pre-crucifixion scenario –
I sit there in bed for an hour and a half – waiting
Before being wheeled at speed down corridors
To the day-procedure operating theatre.

In position, I can see the Great Consultant –
His back. He does not deign to greet me
But in his blue scrubs stands with his back to me
At a counter, mugging up his notes,
Or, as he would pompously snigger, 'consulting your
    files'.
Finally, he spins around on his heel,
Vaunting a glimpse of boyhood's homoerotic hips,
A young middle-aged, grey-haired, baby-faced gang
    boss
Who theatrically thinks of himself as the nurses
Think of him: as a God of the Hospital
(They refer to him never by name – only as HE).
Standing over me he gloats and glowers,
Informing me of the type of anaesthetic I'll be injected
    with.
I ask him a question, but he ignores me – after all,
He is a consultant and consultants do not consult,
Certainly not with a patient.
And so I am injected and a masked nurse
Clamps my mouth, and the Great Consultant
Shoves a sewer rod down my throat
And fifteen minutes later I am trolleyed back to the
    cubicle.
No, this tight-bottomed, pint-sized, Dublin suburbanite
With his Dublin 4 Great Medical Family pedigree –
His Rugby or his GAA field cred –
All-Ireland Championship medals or Irish caps –
Will not be doing any consulting with me today.
A boorish, contemptuous, conceited bully boy.

Three hours later, as I am departing Reception,
He passes me by, pretending not to recognise me.
But I put a spanner in his swagger and greet him and
   compel him
To say 'Ah, Mr Durcan!' and I say to him:
'Do you know what? You are a perfunctory little bugger,
But you have just done me for 600 euro – enjoy!'

The W. B. Yeats Shopping Centre

This morning I visited the W. B. Yeats Shopping Centre
For the first time in my tiny little life.
Although it was built thirteen years ago
I was averse to conferring on it my carbon footprint.

I revelled in it.
How W. B. Yeats also would have revelled in it;
A vast, Babylonian, Celtic Tiger ziggurat
Of so many storeys, so many malls
With millions of women, young and old,
Behind the open-plan counters and stand-alone
    checkouts
But scarcely a single customer –
Scarcely a single consumer except for myself!

And these millions of women, young and old –
Not only were they seriously glamorous
But they were seriously attentive,
Helpful, thoughtful, courteous even!
I spent two hours
Skipping up and down the escalators,
Crooning 'Hug A Shady Wet Nun',
Mooching about,
Pretending to be a customer
And asking advice and getting it –
But, of course, not purchasing anything.

49

Oh, Pasha, but I've been so –
So solo, so to speak –
For the last seven years –
But two hours in the W. B. Yeats Shopping Centre
And I am a new soul!
Poleaxed with adrenalin!
'Revitalised,' as Mrs George Yeats might murmur.
I say to myself:
In the name of Mrs George Yeats –
The most virtuoso housewife who ever lived –
I must purchase something!
I could feel W. B.Yeats egging me on:
He was intoning: 'Obey your urge.'

So, in The House of Harun Al-Rashid,
In the Luggage Department,
I purchased a suitcase with wheels.
Medium-size. Scarlet-red.
Toilet-trained. Guaranteed.
The Cleopatra-like woman
At the checkout batted her eyelashes
And, purring, snapped: '70 per cent off.'
I could see that she considered me
An astute – as well as comely – male consumer.
I sauntered out of her Luggage Department
Talking to my brand-new, scarlet-red suitcase on
      wheels
As if it were my own dog – an Irish wolfhound –
I'd owned for donkey's years.

I cried out to the first passer-by on the street:
'I am a bare-breasted warrior of Erin!'
She — for she also was a she —
We were no longer in Armenia —
(Are the men of Ireland
All up on top of Mount Ararat
Hiding under their motor cars?)
She whispered back to me:
'Where'd you pick up your fancy luggage, Mister?'
I peered down the wells of her eyes,
Dropping my brown pennies down into them:
'In the W. B. Yeats Shopping Centre.'
She stopped in her tracks and stared at me:
'Thank you, sir!' — she screamed at me — 'Thank
    you, sir!'
In the outdoor car park of the W. B. Yeats Shopping
    Centre
I sat down under a recycling bin and wept — wept for joy
and ecstasy and grief and anguish and the whole jing bang
lot and Moses and Isabel Gilsenan and Johannes Scotus
Eriugena and Georgie Hyde-Lees and Eimear McBride
and Robert Heffernan and Katie Taylor and Christine
Dwyer Hickey and Mo Farah and Roisin O'Brien and Joe
Canning and Máire Logue and Rory and Columbanus and
Enda and Fionnuala and Jorge Mario Bergoglio and Michael
D. Higgins and — and — and — and — and — and — and —
and — SABINA!

The Azores High

The women who present the weather forecast on
  Irish TV –
Jean Byrne, Evelyn Cusack, Siobhán Ryan, Nuala
  Carey –
Are the modern-day successors
To the music-hall cabaret singers of the late nineteenth
  century,
Whom we see in the paintings of Manet, Sickert,
  Degas:
The top echelon in Paris and London.
The doyenne of them all is without question Jean
  Byrne,
Although Siobhán Ryan in short-sleeve scarlet frock
Gives Jean Byrne a close run for starry mystique –
Her deep-sea, coming-up-for-air disclosures –
Her swivelling-in-profile-to-camera closing-shot
  technique –
Her pigtail drooling down one bare left shoulder.
Men as well as women race home from work to catch
Jean Byrne's weather forecast at the end of the Six
  One News.
What a luxury it is to lie back on your own sofa
After a long, mindless day's work as Secretary General
Of the Department of Going Forward or Acting Head
  of Going Backwards,
Kick off your slip-on, official black shoes

And watch Jean Byrne perform her latest forecast –
Revealing to you – and you alone – the state of the
    cosmos,
Its innermost secrets, its most intimate details:
'There's a cold front approaching from the east . . .
Yet at the same time approaching from the west
There is an associated suggestion of an Azores High
North-west of Madeira and Porto Santo
Over Newfoundland and Labrador
That might – just might – be coming our way . . .
Reading 10 to 15 hectopascals . . .
But – let's look now at our rainfall predictive
    sequence . . .
A pretty even distribution of showers for this
    evening . . .'
Last night in her body-hugging, all-black, belted silk
    dress
Slit with a sash of lavender-pink,
Her chunky silver necklace and bracelets,
Her block-glass earrings,
She turned her back on you to scan her chart.
Noel, one of our security men – a roly-poly little man
Staring out the porter's office window – sighs:
'They say she's got a huge male following.'

This evening you gaze up at her on the thirty-two-inch
    plasma
Over the fireplace –
Black, sleeveless, zipper-pocketed, denim shirt
Studded with pearl-white buttons

Over bottle-green, skin-tight denim jeans –
A Waterford glass bracelet on her left wrist –
As, caressing her zapper – *her* remote –
She turns around or half-around,
Keeping one eye on her audience – *you* –
And one eye on her weather chart behind her.
When she hits a high note with 'cold front'
In her school-girl contralto
It's like a pillow for your mind!
She bats her eyelashes and she splashes you
With mascara and eyeliner
And her scarlet lipstick smearing your white shirt
    collar,
Like your late mother's homemade raspberry jam,
Until at the climax of her meteorological chanson
She looks you straight in the eye, daggers,
Four-square, and, pausing her pause, she whispers:
'Tonight will be another damp and humid night –
Tomorrow another hot day, but a little hazier in the
    north-west –
With somewhat even hotter conditions during the
    weekend:
I'll leave you with your summary chart, goodnight,
    take care.'

The Gynaecologist at Sixty-Eight in Fitzwilliam Square

Examining a seventy-five-year-old woman of film-star
    beauty and Gypsy dignity
The gynaecologist at sixty-eight is perturbed to become
    aware within himself
Of stirrings of – 'No, no, no, no . . . !
It is unthinkable, as well as improper – pull yourself
    together, old man!'
Yet nonetheless he hears himself saying at the
    termination
Of the consultation how much he admires her long
    wine-red skirt
And even more especially how her transparent
    bottle-green tights
So superbly match her bottle-green patent leather shoes.

After she has gone, alone in his vast, spotless, Donegal-
    carpeted, cream-painted consulting room,
The gynaecologist at sixty-eight is aware of irksome
    feelings of loss and frustration,
Of pining for that seventy-five-year-old woman who
    only minutes ago
Undressed for him before the looking glass – her
    seventy-five years

Naked and raw and coruscating before his gaping
    mouth,
His tongue curling around itself in saliva, and he
    knowing
How hyper-aware she is of her sensual attraction to a
    male of the species.

Dabbing his eyes with his Brown Thomas silk
    handkerchief,
He reaches for the bottle of Bell's Old Scotch in
    the medicine cabinet
And pours himself a large, neat whisky
And empties it down his goosy throat corseted in its
    school-tie cravat
And, chuckling, shakes his head
At the sudden occurrence of such a surprising defeat,
That nevertheless contained within itself
The seed – or seeds, were they? – of victory. On his
    second whisky
He determines on calling her on his new mobile
    smartphone
But on the third whisky he thinks better of it –
'Yes . . . hmm . . . yes . . . such a startling reversal, such
    a bloody awful, totally unexpected, absolutely
    overwhelming, brutally crushing defeat!'

The Killing of Marie Colvin

(d. 22 February 2012)

I

1959 in a tiny public park in New York on a sunny
   morning
A big bald guy in a tracksuit, hands on hips,
His two-and-three-quarters-year-old daughter scooting
   around him.
Already she has mastered the art of the scooter with
   authority.
Two and three-quarters and she cannot put a foot wrong
In her pink-and-orange windcheater, blue jeans, white
   plimsolls,
Her fair hair flying behind her, blue eyes gleaming,
And when she has done she does not throw down her
   scooter –
She parks it at the kerb and puts her hands over her eyes
To try and discern the shape and substance of her father.

II

2012 in a cocktail bar in Beirut, Lebanon,
Two middle-aged women perch on high stools at the bar,
Weighing up the pros and cons of taking up the offer
To cross over into Syria by a smuggler's route,
Bringing them into the heart of the massacre in the city
   of Homs.

Lindsey Hilsum, than whom there is no war reporter
   more honest
Or courageous or wise – weighing it all up –
Considers that the risk is too great, that even the
   great duty
Of reporting the massacre of civilians in Homs
Cannot justify going to what looks like one's own
   certain death.

Marie Colvin mutters, 'You're goddamn right, Lindsey,'
Swirls the swizzle stick in her rum and coke,
Adjusts the yellow curls on the nape of her neck,
Inserts her little finger into the band of her black
   eyepatch,
Grins at her cherished friend, sighs 'I'm off –
See you next week on these same two stools, all right?'

III
Seven days later in a firestorm of government shelling,
By command of His Excellency, President Bashar al-Assad,
In the Baba Amr quarter of the city of Homs in Syria,
Marie Colvin, aged fifty-six, lies mortally wounded,
Spilling her blood and guts alongside a headless child,
Her last heard words, her last known words:
'Why have we been abandoned by the world?'
Her shoes in the hallway alone surviving her killers.
Back in Beirut in an impasse high on a cliff, Lindsey
   Hilsum
Tries to keep walking on, her angered-out eyes placating
   no one.

In the Dublin Mountains

Every time they find skeletal remains in the Dublin
   Mountains
I wonder if it might be — just might be . . .
But it never is! Oh, Alpho —
When will you ever come back to me?

26 February 2012

Early Sunday morning, empty suburban street,
Terminating in aged massive chestnut tree,
Stark, bare, black,
Until close up to it I behold it change before my eyes
Into a maternity hospital seething with childbirth:
Buds breaking their waters, all streaming, all sticky:
Up out of them, evolving without eyes or mouths or
    limbs,
Torsos of naked white embryos with wispy grey hairs.

In rapture of shock I stand back, staring up at the tree
    top,
Its thousands of white skulls blossoming.
I cry out to a little plump government minister being
    driven past:
'Drive on, you self-serving chancer! You're not wanted
    here
Among women and children and passers-by!'

The Dingle Peninsula

It was the Dingle Peninsula that killed him –
He was that happy there.

Arriving late on a Wednesday afternoon
He left early on the Saturday morning.
Yet in those three days and three nights
He caught glimpses of Tír na nÓg:
Of what life might – ought be like:
Of a bed by a window by water,
Of an estuary of trawlers and seagulls,
Of an eagle mountain across the water,
Of narrow winding streets on a hill,
Of a sanctuary harbour built on reclaimed land,
Of a thousand cafés, churches, bookshops,
Of a coastal-path home called 'Cooleen',
Of bluebells and wild garlic;
Of a muezzin alarm clock from Damascus,
Of cloud formations of minarets and onion domes;
Of an adjacent factory called BANG BANG TEO,
Of light beacons at night in the water
Flashing green-red, red-green,
Of gaps in the encircling hills
All leading back to far distant shores,
Of a ninety-year-old, blue-haired lady from Lake
    Wobegon
'Where the women are strong, the men good-looking,

And the children more than average' –
Of a Frenchman with his Irish wife
Letting go of the dolphin,
Of carefree, serious women, young and old,
Of affectionate, humorous, serious men,
Of brazen, mustachioed, middle-aged rascals;
Of pragmatic young dreamers,
Of families changing funerals into festivals,
Of the Irish language being spoken as if it were
    normal
To speak Irish in the streets of an Irish town;
Of Irish and English being spoken in the same
    conversation,
Even in the same sentence.

He found it hard not to think he was back in
    Africa,
In the tribal lands of Mandela's childhood;
Back in that Garden of Eden in the Transkei,
Playing with the other boys and girls,
Before his father smoked his last pipe and died
And the long, silent walk with his mother
Across the mountains to another world:
Within an hour of his being there he knew
That the Dingle Peninsula was an African kingdom
And that the people of Corca Dhuibhne were
    Xhosa –
' . . . with an expressive and euphonious language
And an abiding belief in the importance
Of laws, education, and courtesy'.

62

Hop into the car there –
A retired Mandela policeman said to him;
Up hill and down dale they drove
In the gorse boreens and the stone and the bog
Of Moriarty Territory,
Until they came back down into the plain
To a miniature chapel called the Gallarus Oratory –
A dry-stone, corbelled, ninth-century roof –
Miniature yet vaster than St Peter's Basilica.

'Contains all of the cosmos' –
That's what the first man to walk on the moon
Neil Armstrong
Thought when he first walked into the Gallarus
    Oratory
Forty years after he had walked on the moon.
That's what he thought, that's what he thought:
Instead of feeling he had to say something,
He shook his head, smiling. He shook his head,
    smiling.

In a restaurant called 'An Canteen'
In Dykegate Lane
He ate with a tribeswoman
Of grace and elegance – Úna Fada;
The early morning lift
Was from a daughter called Lasariona,
With a laughing soul and a fold-up bike in her boot;
She talked of nothing but mountains, mountains,

And the brown, brown, brown, brown,
Brown faces of the Sherpa in Nepal;
She dropped him off at the peninsula border.

Outside the train station he stood like the black-and-
    white ghost
Of Sir Roger Casement in the dock,
Waving farewell to her –
Lasariona –
Long after she had disappeared from view.
Back in Dublin city, bereft,
In the badlands,
Underneath the bankrupt hulk
Of the *Clipper Faith*,
Flying the Liberian flag,
Its abandoned crew
Of seventeen Russians and Ukrainians,
He walked the empty, edgy quays
Under the cranes and the gantries
Back to his docklands cave.

He was that happy there –
It was the Dingle Peninsula that killed him.

October, Sunday Morning, Dublin, Ireland

Know that we fools, now with the foolish dead,
Died not for flag, nor King, nor Emperor –
But for a dream, born in a herdsman's shed,
And for the secret Scripture of the poor.

Thomas M. Kettle

This golden-leaved, October Sunday morning, sauntering
with David Rieff
Into a world of 'uncreated light',
In which a young girl can be strangled by Father Life in
broad daylight
In St Stephen's Green, stopping and starting, swans,
ducks and drakes,
Pavilion, bandstand, fountain, statue, pond, bridge, arch,
We saw from afar all alone in the drenched, glistening
grass
Seven Bosnian women pow-wowing in a circle,
cross-legged,
Their faces half-hidden by headscarves and shawls,
Their bent bodies swaddled in many-coloured skirts and
jackets.
One of them stood up and stepped out of the grass
onto the path
To announce to us that she'd no money.

As we foostered in our pockets like two millionaire
     cavemen,
David asked her: 'What are you doing?'
'*Oh Monsieur!*' she laughed merrily. '*Women's Business!*
Where are our Families?'

Adjacent to them on a tall plinth a bust of Signor
     Giacomo Joyce
Stood sentinel, his back to them,
Bejewelled fingers thinking hard on the whole knotty
     problem,
The 'silver-veined, cloistral prose' of John Henry
     Newman,
Humming a new hymn of him, 'Our Lady, Seat
     of Wisdom',
Staring through black railings and gold-green,
     auburn-ochre, terracotta trees
At the Byzantine, blue-and-red hymen of the porch into
     Newman's Barn Church.

Forever and a day, six feet deep,
In St Stephen's Green St Stephen sings:
'Watching the needleboats at San Sabba –
No more, return no more!':
'*O Monsieur!*' she laughed merrily. '*Women's Business!*
Where are our Families?'

Irish Bankers Shoot Dead
Fifty-Seven Homeless Children

'It was great gas – while it lasted,'
Sniffed Vladimir O'Muldowney,
The CEO of the Irish Bankers Gang,
As he snorted a line in the Members Bar of the
    national parliament,
After having shot dead fifty-seven homeless children
In the streets of centre-city, downtown Dublin.
'It was really cool watching the little feckers
Begging us for mercy
And I felt just good and proper and neat and cosy,
My regular mind replete with the right music,
"Britannia, Britannia, Britannia rules the waves!"
(The Lions had beaten the shite out of the All Blacks
    earlier),
Slowly waving my Glock about in the air,
Before picking the little feckers off at random: one, two,
    three.
Every half-dozen of them I'd terminate – I'd pause
And scratch my groin and Skype my better half on
    my iPad
And tell her to sixty-nine me over the phone,
Which of course she was only too willing to do –
Asinine bimbo that she is –
I give her 20K a week for boutique moolah

The 2016 logo of Brand Ireland will be
In fake, high-end Celtic calligraphy:
FUG OV
Signed on Behalf of the Provisional Government
THE OLD HAG OF BEARE

Lady Mayo

Twenty-six years ago on the Westport–Dublin train
    I had a vision of you;
Somewhere between Claremorris and Athlone
    In the over-crowded coach somebody was shining:
How can I forsake you, ever, Lady Mayo?

In a blue denim mini-dress and a yellow denim jacket
               you shone
    Forth far up the coach in an aisle seat;
So that maybe I could say I gave you a lift,
    I invited you to share my taxi and you did:
How can I forsake you, ever, Lady Mayo?

You, whom I have glimpsed the far side of the Mall
    Or in The Blue Bicycle Tea Rooms in Newport,
At the corner of Sunnyside through my silted-up eyes
    I watch you tilting at the water's edge:
How can I forsake you, ever, Lady Mayo?

'Hey, Mr Seaweed Man!' you cry,
    'I have never seen such mustard-yellow seaweed in
        my life!'
Although it was not I who in bare blotched feet
    Coaxed up for you all these sea mammals of kelp:
How can I forsake you, ever, Lady Mayo?

In the Helm bar back on Westport Quay,
  Under photographs of John MacBride and Maud
    Gonne,
We eat a supper of sole and turbot
  And many-coloured *boules* of ice cream:
How can I forsake you, ever, Lady Mayo?

Outside in the night air, your eyes smiling through
  your hair,
  You begin to run – to stride out to the mountain;
Turning only to say to me, 'Rest, breathe, sleep,'
  Crying out, 'I am but an ordinary, breakable,
    workaday woman!'
How can I forsake you, ever, Lady Mayo?

Sea-Haze (Portnakilly Pier, Clare Island)

after Veronica Bolay

She laps up mist. Why
Does she lap up mist
Insatiably? She
Is in high good form
On days of mist.

'I like mist because
In mist you can
See things

And black currachs on the slip
In mist have
Gunwales of gilt.'

26 July 2013

Uncle Willie Montgomery
Dies at 101

Now a wee bit shrunken in the Great Walnut Bowl,
But still the choicest, the shiniest, the reddest, the most
  roguish cherry of them all.

17 December 2012

Heather

At a dinner party in the United States Ambassador's
    Residence
In the Phoenix Park on a summer's evening in the
    mid-1990s
I found myself seated beside Heather Mitchell,
The outgoing young wife of Senator George Mitchell,
To whom Ambassador Kennedy Smith had
    introduced me.
Heather was a conversation-maker as well as a looker.
When everybody moved out and into the lounge
Heather and I sat on at our table, engrossed in chatting
About life, love and literature among the littered
    napkins.
Suddenly I observed Senator George Mitchell hovering
    over us.
Glaring at me, he took her by the hand and uttered,
From the command centre of his ego: 'Heather, let
    us go.'
That was seventeen years ago. A Washington
    correspondent writes:
'Do you realise you could have destroyed the Peace
    Process with your libido?'

Turkish Woman in a Bay Window in Dublin, Winter Coming On

Seated opposite a Turkish woman in a bay window
Of a hotel bar off Merrion Square in October daylight,
Discussing matters on which her advisors
Had thought I might possibly throw light –
Irish Archaeology, Moone, Newgrange –
I dreamed myself a fly on the wall
Instead of the old stick-in-the-mud that I am,
So that instead of spouting like a burst water pipe
I could concentrate, as on a violin concerto,
Wholly on her pleasant expression.
For, indeed, in their briefing-email, her advisors had
    stated:
'She has a most pleasant expression.'
Still, in spite of my tongue hopping up and down,
I was able to compose myself sufficiently to see
The extraordinary significance of what I had been
    forewarned:
'She has a most pleasant expression.'

A woman wholly in tune with her surroundings,
No matter how foreign to her as they were in this
    instance –
She being a Turkish woman, in Dublin, Ireland.
No, not Dublin, Brazil; not Dublin, France;

Not Dublin, Texas, but Dublin, Ireland.
Out of her eyes gazing believingly at me
As I described Professor M. J. O'Kelly
In 1972 at Newgrange
Across the river from Rossnaree
Radiocarbon-dating it to 3,500 years B.C.,
Revealing the winter solstice light box over the
    entrance,
All of her infancy, childhood, girlhood, womanhood!
What noble parents she must have had!
And I asked her: 'Where – where exactly
In Turkey are you from?'
'Zonguldak,' she replied, 'Zonguldak.'
'Zonguldak,' I repeated after her in disbelief.
'I have never before in my life
Met a woman from Zonguldak!'
'Yes,' she sighed fortissimo, 'Zonguldak
Is a city on the Black Sea,
On the south coast of the Black Sea,
Very noteworthy for its coal mines;
It is about three hours by auto from Istanbul.
You, I think' – she observed, leaning across our
    table –
'You would like very much Istanbul.'
'Oh, I am sure I would,' I affirmed,
'But I think I might like even more
Some day to visit *you* in Zonguldak!'
After a suitable silence, a fruitful silence,
Having each of us digested our words,
She smiled inaudibly and I smiled inaudibly, too,

Remembering a thinking man I knew once in Trieste
Whose name was Claudio.
'What date is it today?' I asked her.
'The twenty-sixth of October,' she enlightened me.
'You know,' I said, 'Delius stated that music
Is but the imparting of spiritual unity to one's thoughts.'
'Yes,' she murmurs, 'Zonguldak!'
'Yes,' I murmur, 'Zonguldak!'
It is so regrettable to have to say goodbye.
Is life too high a price to pay for death?
I cry: 'In Ireland it is too dark! Goodbye!'
She cries: 'Come to Asia Minor where there is light!
   Goodbye!'

My Quiet Man

It was when he used have to go away,
Betimes as far as Australia, Japan, Brazil,
Four times to Newfoundland,
That I used think our life together was over
Or almost over,
But then on the morning of his return
After two or three weeks or even a month
I'd collect him at the airport
And as we drove home
Everything was so calm – almost wordless –
Between us.
Then, in the hall, he'd put down his bags
On the stone flags
And after we'd embraced for an eternity
We'd process slowly – ever so slowly – upstairs
To my bedroom
Overlooking the copper beech older than the house,
And what would happen then –
Lasting for at least two or three hours –
Is something I cannot tell you about,
Except to say:
Have you ever heard the drumming of the jack snipe
In the mating season in the Bogs of Erris?
O my Lord God of Erris! The drumming of the jack
    snipe!
My quiet man!

Lullaby of an Unmarried Mother

No, no, I'd not like to be a married mother!
And to think that not so long ago in Ireland
If I were an unmarried mother
They'd have locked me up
Or taken away my child from me!
Of course, if a girl
Wants to be a married mother
That's her feckin prerogative, you might say,
But personally speaking
Being an unmarried mother is feckin ideal.
How uncool it would be
To have a feckin man in the house!
Excepting, of course, my father.
(My father's a dote —
Still driving his taxi.)
But men, generally speaking,
Are a feckin encumbrance, you might say.
No, take it from me, Shirley,
Be an unmarried mother
Living at home with your parents:
You'll have a whirly time with your kid
And in the evenings you'll be free.
What class of a girl would not want
To be an unmarried mother?
A Pearl of the Coombe, you might say.
I wake in the feckin morning and listen

To my three-year-old daughter
In her bunk bed beside me
Talking to herself – what could be cosier,
So convenient,
And – more to the feckin point – more
    economical?

Portrait of a Risk-Taker in her Seventy-Second Year

No greater audacity hath a woman in her
    seventy-second year
Than on the evening before the dawn flight on Delta
From Dublin to Florida via Atlanta
And a week with her old friend Patience in Sarasota,
To drive to the aid of an old boy in distress,
Paying not only the energy price and the psyche price,
But 120 euro for the privilege of being clamped.

It was precisely 3.30 p.m. on a chilly afternoon in
    March
When after she had driven six or seven miles to my
    aid,
In her typical fashion without fuss or blackmail,
As I trotted back with her to her car
She cursed: 'Oh! No! They've clamped me!'
On the front right wheel of her red Renault
The grotesque yellow plate of the clamper –
The clamper's swastika – symbol of all
That is male, rapacious, lewd, genocidal.

As I am the proximate cause of this act of barbarity
I tell her how sorry I am – only for her
To tell me to forget it and go away and leave her
    alone,

Muttering 'I'll sort it out' and looking up at me
    smiles,
Saying 'I was always a risk-taker.'

At 6.45 p.m. she responds to my email:
'Yes, I am sitting here on sofa wrapped up in red rug,
Sipping hot whiskey with lemon and cloves,
Looking at the news – Cork politician on conspiracy to
    murder,
Foiled murder in Londonderry, real murder done
In faraway Tokyo – as I ponder my last-minute bits and
    bobs
For the orange groves and blue skies of Sarasota . . . '

Will she sleep? Does she sleep? Can she sleep?
At 5 a.m. the taxi picks her up for the airport.
At 8.35 a.m. she is airborne – she is flying
West south-west – reading
Tuesday morning's *Daily Telegraph*,
Their chief art critic Richard Dorment's banner
    headline
Over Manet's *The Railway*:
MAKING US SEE THINGS DIFFERENTLY.
Smiling at the spectacle of Manet, she dozes.
'I was always a risk-taker.'

Life is Too Short

When you're a female vet for a leading horse trainer
You need to take as many breaks as you can –
If you know what I mean. Life is too short.
With my friend Aisling every October early
We go to Spain.
Last year Marbella – four-star hotel for five days –
130 euro return Cork–Marbella. For nothing!
Average mean temperature 26 degrees.
This year Barcelona – the same,
Just a little bit cooler – 22 degrees.
Oh, but we had so much fun in Barcelona.
Another four-star hotel in the city centre,
The old city centre.
It was such a howl. Howl-arious!
Aisling is mad for the sangria in the morning.
At 10.30 she's already in the café
In that loose, low-cut, scarlet, mini-frock she favours:
'My belly-and-rump number,' she calls it.
'José!' she is howling. '*Una sangria por favor!*'
To Aisling they're all José in Barcelona.
Whatever the café, the waiter is always José.
Of course, sangria is scrumptious, but it's deadly:
Pure alcohol in pure fruit juice.
So that by lunchtime
I have to give her a piggyback
Back to our bedroom.

We share a king-size bed – it's practical
And, besides, it's quite nice
Waking up beside a girlfriend.
We play like kittens.
But she's a strong girl, Aisling,
Same age as myself, forty-seven,
And after a siesta
That would knock out a rhinoceros
She's ready for the pool
And her rum and coke
And her coffee – real coffee.
Oh, we're very coffee snobs.
We don't like Starbucks.
No. No, no. No, no, no. No.
We spent a whole week in Barcelona
With the sangria mornings
And the rum and coke afternoons
And devouring chunks of Gorgonzola
And getting toasted on our sunbeds,
And Aisling, bellowing
At poolside
As if she owned the poor *hombre*,
'José! José! *Por favor! Por favor!*'
And one day who did we see but Connie Murphy
From the Castlemartyr Stud
And he in the nip!
Oh, the cut of him!
Fancies himself in the nip!
He has gone into receivership –
Serves him right!

Massaging his ego, took his eye off the ball!
Like them all!
Aisling – and as I say she's forty-seven also –
She's Head Lad in the yard
And there's not a trainer in Ireland
Who would not give his Y-fronts to have Aisling.
She's that amazing with horses
And she's only been kicked six or seven times
In her whole life!
I've been kicked hundreds of times.
When I was twenty, a mad mare
Near broke my neck. Look! Look!
The scar under my bra! Do you see it?
Anyway, next month it's Jordan.
Great five-night deals in five-star hotels in Aqaba.
Aisling of Arabia!
Life is too short.

Laragh Man
at the funeral of Ian Stuart, sculptor

'My mother was the first great love of my life –
The first woman I paid court to' –
He used say, who, today, aged eighty-six –
St Valentine's Day –
In sunshine and rain
Was lowered down
Into his mother Iseult Gonne's
Grave in a casket of wickerwork
With pots of snowdrops
And a bouquet of twelve white tulips:
In the narrow grave whose granite headstone –
After their daughter Siobhán was slain
In a car crash aged thirty-five –
Was carved by his first wife Imogen
In the style of the early Celtic stelae
With a tiny window in it, sheltering a sparrow.

His mother reared and raised him in Laragh in Glendalough
With his sister Katherine and his father Francis Stuart,
And when he married his first wife he brought her back
To his mother's home in Laragh.
After his mother's death he made his own home
In Laragh with his second wife Anna and his thousands
Of daughters and granddaughters and great-granddaughters,
And in another country the women he did not marry

And their daughters. At the funeral service,
Amidst candlelit black lanterns and pots of snowdrops,
There was a large black-and-white portrait photograph
Standing at the head of the open casket:
The sculptor in his forties,
A silent, brooding, sultry fusion
Of the young Marlon Brando and the young Boris
    Pasternak.
'An artist of great style and promise,
But he stood almost alone in his generation,'
Wrote Brian Fallon,
The pre-eminent critic of the time.
You could say that many women not only liked
But loved this man
Or that he was a man who not only liked
But loved many women:
And to a woman
All the women were saying
At his graveside
That what their man
Most wanted to have been
Was to have been a monk –
A Benedictine!

By the Sign of Contradiction
In Glendalough graveyard
With his daughter in his arms –
Laragh Man, asleep in his mother's grave.

14 February 2013

A Husband Nattering to His Wife

Technically Margery died three years ago,
But to Robert she is not dead –
At worst, she is, perhaps, 'missing'
Or more likely, simply, 'away' –
'Away on one of those jaunts of hers, you know,
With her girlfriends – things and places
Chaps would never know anything about.'
He opens her wardrobe in their bedroom
And with his back to the wardrobe
While he makes the bed he natters to her:
'I do like your polka-dot green-and-red frock,
But the one I like you best in is the plain yellow
    frock –
The plain yellow frock is most *you*.'
He picks up her pair of low-heeled brown brogues
And stands them up in the fireplace.
'You look almost perfect in the low heels –
Somehow the high heels are too high for you – and me.
Margery, will you come for a drive this afternoon?
I know you think I am too old to drive,
But really I am as handy at the wheel
As ever I was – if there is a problem
It's the other drivers that are the problem.
Come on, darling, let's, let's drive up the hills
To Ticknock or the Three Rock,
But first I'll make us a little lunch.

Would you like a bowl of oxtail or salad or both?
And a peppermint tea with – yes – with two sugars?
Yes, yes, that's my girl Margery, oh yes
Let's be spousal, all-out, this afternoon – and tonight!
Why, tomorrow let's drive over to the Phoenix Park
And you will lean on the white rails of the cricket
  ground
While I go down on my knees before you with my
  camera –
For that is all I want – or ever really wanted – in this
  life to do –
With my camera to go down on my knees before you,
  my beloved, my irrepressible wife,
The obelisk of the Wellington Monument behind us
  plunging up into red-hot cloud,
And in the sun-room of their home opposite us
President Michael D. Higgins and his wife Sabina –
"Those thousand little flowers" that "obdure in a wild
  place" –
Reading poetry to one another in order to stay sane.
Isn't it the hardest thing of all to stay sane?
There is only one way in Nova Scotia and Cape Breton
  to stay sane
And that is to read poetry to one another.
Tonight, Margery, I will drink a glass of water to thee.'

Sea Coast at Trouville 2012

Throwing on a threadbare hot-pink frock –
He'd like it, I thought –
'Chic slumming' he'd call it –
I picked it up in a charity shop –
Three euro – THREE EURO! –
I swung out the town to the cliff.
There he was, punctilious as always,
Poised in profile, one eye
To the ocean, one eye to the cliff:
A most parfait knight, Claude.
(His name is Paul, but we had signed a treaty
In Versailles
Whereby I might always call him Claude.)
Before he caught sight of me I knew
Exactly why it was I could never sleep
With him, why we could never be lovers –
Much less companions under one roof,
What I knew he was yearning for.
What kind of girl could live
With all that yearning, all
Those roots of parsnips in her eyes?
He was fifteen years older than me,
But that was not what stood in our way;
Indeed, I took pleasure in the age difference,
In those 'Round Cape Horn' fifteen years.
No, it was simply because of how he looked

And who and what he was.
Gallant, hilarious, striking,
In café or salon or ballroom
No monsieur more congenial than he,
But here on the ocean at the cliff edge
There was nothing – but nothing –
Earthly about him.
All divinity he was, all poetry.
Before I smiled and waved to him
I recognised him for what he was:
An old ghost of a thorn tree
Blasted to bits by black salt gales.
From a woman's point of view – an autistic elk!
Utterly aesthetic, utterly unlivable with.
If I was but to surrender once to him
He'd be my scapegoat for evermore
And what woman with a *centime* of heart
Would want that?
Cher Claude, au revoir.

The Man of Advancing Years and the Girl on a Bicycle

A man of advancing years, about ten years younger
    than myself,
Is turning right at the lights in his two-door,
    metallic-silver Ford Fiesta –
'Making a right', as they drawl stateside –
From Grand Canal Street into Clanwilliam Place,
While a cyclist is taking her time on her pedals
    pedantically,
Being young, carefree, nonchalant, emitting femininity.
In frustration, at first he brandishes his right arm
But concurrently, in a tantrum, he clenches his veiny,
    mottled fist,
Glaring over at me at my wheel for male moral support:
'No siree!' – I smile – 'No siree!
Did you not learn at your potted, privileged, exclusive,
Fee-paying, Holy Ghost boarding school long ago
That the girl on a bicycle always takes precedence?
Always the not-yet pregnant Mother of God?'

The Twenty-Four-Hour Piano Recital

'Where are you going?' she asked me.
I replied: 'I am walking you to your car.'
Seeming almost to mutter, she remonstrated: 'No need
    for that!'
She – a woman of particular manners, particular affections;
A woman of a lifetime of hard work and undiluted
    leisure.
When we got to her car, I opened the driver's door:
She glanced up at me, almost glaring at me:
'I am not used to men opening doors for me.'
She climbed in, putting her head down to insert the
    ignition key
And, surplus to requirements, I crawled away.
Above me a clutch of pine trees was shaking its head
And around the corner in the doorway of a boutique,
Opposite a boarded-up grocery store,
A lone, bare-headed gentleman
Was xylophoning tears from his eyes,
Pretending otherwise.
A Vale of Tears in the Suburbs of Dublin –
In which there is no escaping
Young, bow-tied Death waiting for all of us around
    the corner,
Sitting upright at his black piano, taking his time,
Sitting upright all day at his black piano,
Sitting upright all night at his black piano,

Turning sideways to smile at us from time to time,
Serenading you 'I'll meet you in Venice at
    Christmas-tide!'
As I drive up and down the switchback suburban hills
Back to my own palazzo of loneliness in the city –
A tearful, crumpled-up, little kip of a shoebox
Behind 'The Ruari Quinns' – the new council housing
    estate,
Named after a petite, goatee-bearded, local politician,
Down the docklands, the River Liffey willing itself out
    into Dublin Bay.
I'll tell you what it is and what it is not:
In the Twenty-Four-Hour Piano Recital in our sixties
I am a dependent man and she is an independent
    woman –
One of the First Realists, one of the Last Romantics.

What Came Squeezing through My Letter Box This Morning

Ten thirty a.m., knock on door.
In my pyjamas I stick my head out the window.
The postman below in the street gapes up at me, yells:
'It's okay, gaffer! I've got it through your box!'
I hear something plopping on the hall floor.
I do a monkey's down the stairs. There on the hall
    floor
Under the taboo aperture in the door
Is a thin, elongated packet – about three-and-a-half
    feet –
Wrapped in brown paper and Sellotaped.
What in the Name of Woman can it be?

Postally speaking – whatever it may be –
It makes the river sit up!
As I begin to slice it open with a nail scissors
As delicately as a surgeon executing a tracheotomy
I note that it has been solicitously swaddled in bubble
    wrap.
Almost immediately I begin to detect the handle of
    a stick.
Inconceivably, that's what emerges
Into the sunlight on the floor – a walking stick!
A malacca cane with an inlaid stone handle.

Out of a sealed white envelope bearing my name
I pluck – no, withdraw – a white card
On which there is a photograph of a grey art card –
The script of Prospero's spellbinding speech in
    The Tempest
Inscribed in black ink in calligraphy:
Our revels now are ended. These our actors,
As I foretold you, were all spirits, and
Are melted into air, into thin air;
And like the baseless fabric of this vision,
The cloud-capped-towers, the gorgeous palaces,
The solemn temples, the great globe itself,
Yea, all which it inherit, shall dissolve;
And, like this insubstantial pageant faded,
Leave not a rack behind. We are such stuff
As dreams are made on, and our little life
Is rounded with a sleep.
Inside the card, a colour photo of the late David Kelly,
Actor, calligrapher.
On the facing page a note in a flowing, generous hand:
We thought it appropriate that you have the 'stick' with
The hope that you won't need it for many a year to come.
Lots of love. The Kellys xx

So! Wow! Who crowed that Ireland is not an enchanted
    isle?
An uninhabited island in the northern oceans?
Have you ever heard of such audacious kindliness?
Have you ever known such corporeal thoughtfulness?

Have you ever known such charity in grief?
Have you ever known such good nature and good
    humour?

Hairy with euphoria I cartwheel across the street —
Almost forgetting to pull on a pair of trousers
Over my pyjamas.
The front door of the good neighbour woman opposite
    is open
But not a creature to be seen.
I throw a fit crying out 'Carla! Carla!'
Carla Daly Kovács, just back on her bike from having taken
Tímea (6) and Zalán (4) to school
Finds herself abruptly, unexpectedly, innocently
On the receiving end of a hysterical outburst
From her moulting, white-haired neighbour across the
    street.
Yet then she also joins in my revelry, my delirious
    revelry,
And her sister Dr Lisa Daly from Houston, Texas, joins us
For morning coffee, tea and cookies and
We toast and sing the person, life, work and family
Of the Kellys — Laurie, David, Miriam and
Their late great husband and father — the Greatest —
The One and the Only — David Kelly,
Actor, calligrapher.
What he most liked to say is true except of himself;
'None of us will be remembered — matter a damn.'

1 September 2012

Nothing Like the Funeral of a Good Man to Lift the Spirits

As I was crossing the street to walk in the church gate
The hearse driver attempted to knock me down.
He looked at me as much as to say:
'Knocking down pedestrians is what I like doing best.'
I brandished my claws at him in pathetic fury:
He spat at me, lighting up a fag.

The deceased was Eddie Spollen –
As ordinary, as decent, as good a man as you'd ever
    meet –
A real working-class Dubliner of the old stock,
Married to Dot (Dorothy) for fifty-five years:
Three sons, nine grandchildren, three great-grandchildren.

Eddie was a metalworker across the bridge
Who worked every day of his life
Until he retired ten years ago:
Always the last man to clock out,
Always the first man to clock in.
The wife and the kids were everything to him,
As well as helping out neighbours
And working for handicapped people
And organising pilgrimages to Lourdes.
Nights he'd go down for the few pints

And the grandchildren would ambush him
On the way back for the small change,
Which he always gave them.

The priest said: 'It was Eddie's ordinariness –
His exceptional ordinariness – his brilliant ordinariness –
That made him a saint – a sarcastic saint!
We'll all miss him terribly –
Most of all his wife Dot and the family,
But all of us who knew him will miss him.
The Lord says somewhere
That the worst thing about death
Is not death itself,
Which after all is quite a big dramatic event –
Not to mention all the other little dramas around it –
No – the worst thing about death is the emptiness –
The emptiness death leaves behind.
That's what the Lord says somewhere in the Gospels
And how right the Lord is.
Next week when we're all finding ourselves
Thinking about Eddie
We're all going to realise how empty a quarter
The world is without Eddie in it –
How bloody empty the world is without Eddie.
Forgive me my altar language. Have mercy on me.
Praise be the Lord. Let's sing the Ave Maria!'

Outside after the Funeral Mass was over,
Among the sympathisers milling around the mourners,

I overheard Maureen Connolly saying
'Wasn't it a lovely Funeral Mass!'

Having kissed the widow and shook hands
With two of the sons and the partner of one of the
    grandsons
I walked to my car to find it had been clamped!
I felt like as if I'd been shot dead through the head.
My *neighbour* (well, that's what she calls herself),
Appraising me from under her rust-dyed tresses,
Shrugged her moth-eaten shoulders and drawled:
'I love to see people getting clamped.'
Yes, that's what she said, so cosy-like, so natural-like, so
    casual-like:
'I love to see people getting clamped.'

Survivor on the Back of the World

after Margaret Morrisson

Although I am a buck-goat
Stranded on the mountaintop
Over the lintel of the universe –
Black fog, visibility zero –
Things could be worse,
As worse today they were
Down in the Georgian quarter
Where I lost my footing –
Oh, these cloven flip-flops of mine! –
Betwixt kerb and pavement
Outside Restaurant Patrick Guilbaud;
Two well-fed government ministers passing by
Adjusted their sunglasses, passing on.

But now in the gutters high up
In the maelstrom of the mountain
Being ogled by flighty thunderstorms
I am safe from apparatchiks.
I am no scapegoat.
I am a survivor,
Butterfly fragile,
But my horns are not for sale:
Each is a sickle
Which I propose
Only to daughters of high birth,

No matter how low
Their station on the mountain.
On a bad day on top of the world
I flash my eyelashes
Back down the corrie
At the she-goat princesses of my daydreams.
PS: If you – dear passer-by –
Happen to be a well-fed government minister –
And you're IN THE MOOD
Throw a black, white and gold rug over me –
That one.
I am proud of my glacier.
That will do. *Merci*.

2 July 2014

A Cure-All for the Black Dog

By appointment this morning at 9.30 a.m. I met the
    Great Psychiatrist
In his rooms at the Mount of Olives Clinic in Dublin 4.
The Great Psychiatrist almost inaudibly said to me:
    'Obviously
I could throw the book at you –
Bipolar – menstrual stress – schizophrenia – hysteria –
    neurasthenia –
And obviously also you are
In grievous need of hugging therapy –
Indeed, seeing as how you are a ravishing Scotswoman
    of sixty-eight –
A Highlands Goddess of the Heroic Age of the Clans –
I'd hug you myself,
Only I'd be in breach of medical ethics
And likely as not to get struck off,
But now in any case what I am going to prescribe
Is a shopping pilgrimage to Belfast.
Myself when I was an eenshy-weenshy little boy
My dystopian mother used go on an annual shopping
    pilgrimage to Belfast.
(Conceited of me, that, isn't it? – "dystopian" mother!
I'm nothing if not the most conceited polecat in Great
    Britain and Ireland.
You see, I simply swoon when I think of all your
    investments and shares,

And indeed, really, the financial holdings of all my most
    cherished patients –
No, not patients, clients. Clients!)
And my dystopian mother always came back the better
    for it
As well as never forgetting to bring back
To her one and only little boykins packets of sweets
    – SPANGLES;
Sweets that you could obtain only in Northern Ireland.
Ravishing although you may be – O my God O
But you really are a Goddess, aren't you? –
Do you realise that you are wearing the same clobber
    today
As when first you consulted me thirty-five years ago?
Do you hear me? I am whispering – no, murmuring – to
    you.
Why are you smiling? By any chance are you smiling
    at me?
Now: I want you to make a day trip to Belfast
On the train, premium class, aisle seat, facing forward.
At Belfast Central you will take a taxi
Straight into the city centre to the Victoria Square
    Shopping Centre
And there you will submit to E.R.T.: Electric Retail
    Therapy.
Item: one forest-green greatcoat buttoned up to the
    collar
(A 2014 design based on Meissonier's history painting
Of Napoleon Bonaparte's stag party of marshals on
    horseback);

One red-and-black hat – a Cloche Trilby with
    turned-down brim;
One pair of suede green-and-black shoes;
Two pairs of teal-green tights;
One Prussian Blue cotton skirt;
One tartan scarf of the clan MacDonald –
Green, blue, black with a thin red line,
Stringy tassels at both ends.
Back in Dublin you will phone up your toy boy
Whom you have not phoned in ages –
How remiss of you –
And you will mobilise him. And he will – he will come
    to you –
Driving like a meteorite up the Grand Canal
From Huband Bridge to Dolphins Barn Bridge
And, tearing off all his thermal vests and thermal long
    johns,
He will curl up at your feet
While you climb all over him
Like, I dare say, a seal on a beach ball.
In point of fact, you will feel like a new woman
At sixty-eight going on sixty-nine.
No pills. No concoctions. No placebos. Pure shopping
    therapy
In the House of Fraser in the heart of Belfast –
The most sumptuous city in the United Kingdom –
At affordable prices in all the gleaming glory of anonymity
And – pure adoration from the forlorn toy boy at your
    feet –
Unconditional surrender!'

The Laughing Receptionist in the GP's Surgery

When I nip into the GP's surgery
To pick up a repeat prescription
For anti-depressants and sleeping pills
I find the fair-haired receptionist
On her elbows with laughter,
For no reason other than that this April
    day
Is all sunlight and blue skies,
Street lined with limes of new green leaf,
Tiny gardens jungles of white magnolia.
She announces: 'Today is the day
For buying a villa on the seafront:
I know I must win the Lottery –
But how can I win the Lottery
When I do not even remember
To buy a Lottery ticket?
And even then, in any case,
I forget to check the results!'
She is weeping with laughter.
I wade out into the street
And not caring if YOU are watching me
I pluck a blue tulip from a front garden,
Wade back in and present it to her.
I, too, am weeping with laughter

As I let myself out of the surgery and –
Dear Mrs Double Parking – I do not give a farthing
What you think – it's spring!

Photograph of Ben with His Baby Son Matteo, Mayo, July 2013

Christmas Infant in high summer
In his French father's lap on a haymaking day
In the Plains of Mayo, the Hidden Ireland:
You have never seen a man
So entranced as Ben –
In his brick-red 'History of the Human Race'
    T-shirt –
Big black sunglasses high in his thinning black hair –
His baby son Matteo
Swaddled in turquoise-and-gold in his lap,
Sleeping the sleep of the deep-sea fields.
That all-embracing, incredulous trance
That only a shy, reticent father can know –
Interrogating himself what on earth he has done
To deserve the Gift of the Infant
Matteo so perfectly wrapped.
He gazes down in pride-embroidered bewilderment
At the fair-haired baby, mouth open, eyes shut,
Lost in sleep, forever lost in sleep,
Leaving behind him his entranced father,
A lost sheep on the green road to the sea,
Crying out, bleating, across the heather, over and over:
Praise be to Matteo's Irish mother, brave Sarah Joyce!

The Mystery of the Incarnation

in memoriam Brendan Tobin

I

It was Christmas Day and we were at our wits' end,
Or almost, wondering how on earth we'd get
   through it,
How on earth we'd survive it –
Not even the turf fire would light –
When out of the blue in the early afternoon
A third man whom I had never set eyes on
Slipped into the day and changed everything.
For hours in a quiet, childlike, older countryman's voice,
Dreamy, indignant, awkward, cheerful, mischievous,
He told story after story, epic after epic, of the Purple
   and Gold,
Of his family, his tribe, his village, his county, his country:
Oulart, the Harrow, Killann, the Duffry, Boolavogue.
He spoke in a low voice rumbling with shy excitement.
About Nicky Rackard he was eager to say something.
About Eileen Gray he did not say anything.

II

When he departed – it was entirely my fault –
The car in which he was a back-seat passenger
Almost knocked me down, backing into me.
It moved off into the night and I looked up

At the stars – the Plough and Orion over the Irish
   Sea –
And then at the car, the back of his turning head,
His squinting eyes – could it have been his eyes also
   were smiling? –
At least one of Orion's shoulders up there appeared to
   be smiling.
The car sped out through the open gate and away.
How could I have known
I would spend the rest of my life thinking of him,
But that I would never see him again?

When he had gone, he left behind him
Mildness, smoothness, gentleness,
A kind of kindred kindness.
It was insisted upon by everyone
That it was the best Christmas by far
In a long, long time – in truth, not since
That Christmas in Newgrange 5,000 years ago
When the sun shone at the winter solstice
Had we seen a Christmas like it.

Visiting Elizabeth at Home

In Beloved Memory: Elizabeth Walsh Peavoy 1945–2014

'Will we sit downstairs or go upstairs?
To tell the truth, I am a little tired.
Shall we go upstairs?
You see, I'm on morphine and I have chemo
   tomorrow.
Mind you, chemo does bump me up.
You don't mind if I get into bed?
Fully clothed, of course!
You can sit on that chair – yes, that one –
No, no, you should never hold a chair like that
By the top – yes, yes,
That's the right way, by the legs;
But that plate in your hands –
Don't leave it turned upside down.
I can see you appraising all of my chaos –
Garments and books strewn all over –
You might not think it but I know
Where everything is – I can find
Anything I want to find. You see
That long orange envelope?
I've all my poems in that!
I wonder if I'll ever write another poem?
I could drop dead anytime
But I don't envisage that.

Madeline died in her sleep after breakfast.
If I could buzz off in the same way.
How am I?
Unmercifully well.
Unmercifully ill.
And then, of course, there is my attic.
You must see my attic. For example,
I have *your* books in my attic.
Oh, you should give up Dublin!
You should go out into the country
And read your great books to the people.
Go to Yaroslavl, go to Gorki, go to the Urals
And beyond, go to Chelyabinsk,
Go to Ballaghadereen and Ballivor and Tully
   Cross.
Go to Abbeyleix.
Get out of that cave of yours!
What's more, it's not a cave − it's a rathole.
You must cease living in a rathole.
Stop fretting about your clutch.
We've all burnt out
A clutch in our time.
My son Tadhg at eighteen
Driving across Canada −
An eighteen-year-old wouldn't be up
To that kind of thing.
The Red Cross gave him wellington boots
And a set of underwear.
In the heart of Manitoba.
The Red Cross put him up in a motel

On the edge of a beauty spot –
A beauty spot with a difference.
The name of the motel –
Can you believe it? –
Fawlty Towers! In Manitoba!
He'd burnt out his clutch.
I had to phone him:
"Letter here for you from TCD –
Will I open it?"
His moving-on papers,
To Theology in Louvain.
Stop fretting about your clutch.
Visiting a friend in the psychiatric ward
Who was in the next bed but my own GP?
With his expected bride-to-be!
I think it was the collywobbles.
He married the woman –
I heard via the grapevine.
I love flowers, don't you?
I lost a glove in the flower shop.
Losing a glove is always a good sign.
My son Eoghan took me
To *Les Misérables* the other day –
Wasn't that sort of sweet of him?
He says that we don't have enough milk
But I say that we do.
"I'm talking to Paul Durcan –
But that's not relevant to you."
Above all, I love frost – most of all the frost I
    can see

Melting on the slates of the roofs the other side
Of the street. Frost is what really gets me going.
But, of course, as Anne says, you have to remember
That *Ulysses* is poetry –
It's what's called the Panoply of Human Experience –
A lot of it may never have happened.
Anne's brother has cancer of the oesophagus.
I found that out from a third party.
According to that source it's not terminal.
Let me show you my morphine pump.
Have you ever seen a morphine pump?
It's what's keeping me alive.
I wouldn't be lying here
Talking to you like this if I didn't
Have my morphine pump.
Come here, up close, closer –
Just above my breast –
My right breast – look!
Don't look so horrified!
It's what's keeping me alive.
Remember me when I was seventeen,
Me and the other girls
Showing off our suspenders
At lunchtime in Dwyer's public house.
"Did a torpedo strike the ship?"
Mother, dead, is very happy.
I had to go to the bank this morning.
Did you know – banks
Are not for people any more?
Still, I said to the girl: "I am meeting

Paul Durcan at two o'clock –
Wouldn't you like to be me?
Of course, you would. I can see the envy
Written all over your face."
The newspaper – did you read
Eileen Battersby on rats?
I always read today's paper tomorrow.
Venus had to give up tennis
Because of rheumatoid arthritis –
That's the latest news.
Sometimes after chemo I feel
Like my cart has got only three wheels
When it should have four wheels.
It's not pleasant – that feeling.
Oh, Antoinette is Irish despite the French name
And now she has this man,
But he wants to lock her away –
Men are like that.
She and I are going to go shopping
For underwear next week.
Nothing like a clean pair of knickers
To pep up the spirits.
Ruth has her pilot, her Air Corps pilot.
They're getting hitched next year.
You might see him
Walking around Sallynoggin.
Can you walk around Sallynoggin?
Diarmuid went to the Ivory Coast last week.
To teach them Democratisation.
He said he'd be back on Thursday.

I wonder will he?
You don't mind letting yourself out?
Put one foot in front of the other
And get on your bike.
The Reverend Mother will pedal.
Kiss me again. Goodbye.
It was nice – us meeting here,
Wasn't it? No tension.
Bye. Bye.'

Breaking News

I was driving up the mountain
Through the fuchsia and the sheep –
Horned black faces –
At 11.30 a.m. in the morning
Of the last Friday in August
When, fingers slipping on the dials,
Clambering out to unbolt the six-barred gate,
I switched on the radio accidentally:
'The death has been announced of the poet Seamus
    Heaney.'
A mist loomed, cloaking each sheep, sheep by sheep,
Shrouding all of the mountain and the western sea.

Inside the house the first chill of autumn.
I block-built a few firelighters in the grate,
Kindling, peat briquettes,
Struck a FIRESIDE safety match, white flames leaping up,
And down the chimney rustled Seamus's antiphonal
Derry brogue (undiluted by Harvard, Berkeley, Oxford,
    the BBC, Carysfort, RTE, Queen's)
'Are you all right down there, Poet Durcan?'
(That's how he always addressed me down thirty-seven
    years –
'Poet Durcan')
'Calm down, I'm only dead, I'm only beginning
The new life, only hours and minutes into it;

I miss my wife, my children, my grandchildren, my
    brothers,
Most of all my mighty spouse – otherwise
I've become the spaceman I've always longed to be –
In flight – breaking the sound barrier out in the
    cosmos –
Which, since boyhood – the American Air Force in our
    fields –
The aerodromes between our hedgerows –
Has always been my dream, my home, my Elysium –
After a lifetime of being neither here nor there –
Of being Kidnapped by Time –
I am out in the cosmos –
Tramping the Milky Way with my father and mother –
Our neighbour Rosie Keenan singing shut-eyed at the
    well –
Tiepolo skies salmon-pink, white, gold beneath our
    feet –
Never getting above ourselves, what it's all about –
Damascus, Athens, Jerusalem, children –
Down there below us, north-west Europe –
Anahorish, Mossbawn, Bellaghy –
Swarms of midges in veiled autumn evening light –
Anna Rose, Aibhín, Síofra – the other world –
And now I put the key for the first time
Into the door of my father's house.'

30 August 2013

The Painter Gustave Caillebotte
Writing to His Brother, 1877

My dear Martial
Provisionally entitled *Paris Street, Rainy Day*
It's a choreography, actually, for umbrellas –
Steel-framed umbrellas.
(That melancholy little Belgian maggot Magritte
Years later nicked the idea from me.)
Puzzle is where to pose the umbrellas.
They're all pricked out, of course, unfurled,
So that their pointed tips – eight per brolly –
Constitute a carousel of arousal
Damped down slightly by lightly falling rain,
All our paving stones in heat:
Don't, don't, Marguerite!
Oh do, oh do, Simon!

I posed them on a promenade in Normandy
But changed my mind, for I wanted also
To compose an ode to people-watching
In the Place de Dublin
At the intersection of the rue de Saint-Pétersbourg
And the rue de Moscou,
The rue de Bucarest and the rue de Turin.
So I catch in the foreground a couple
Glancing with pointed curiosity

At another couple who are out of picture:
'Is not that Monsieur Simon Lagarde
With the young English lady Mrs Marguerite Fox?
They're both married but not to each other.
A wet day for adultery.'
But it is the can-can of the umbrellas
That is my erotic secret –
More erotic even
Than afternoon tea with my neighbour Bertha!
Umbrella Can-Can, Paris 1877 –
What say you?
Your affectionate brother, Gustave Caillebotte.

Dorothy Molloy in UCD on a Thursday Afternoon in May 2007

to Andrew Carpenter

Between the O'Reilly Hall and the Lake,
On the one, solitary, broken, upright bench on the lawn,
In the sun-trap under the National Virus Reference
    Laboratory,

Enthroned, reading a book,
Her orange-sleeved, blue blouse providing a scenic
    backdrop
For two white swans –

Who, after a winter of presiding over their crannóg nest
    in the Lake,
Exploded a week ago into the water
With six chicks –

Dorothy Molloy
Enquires between black clouds, peering out over her
    spectacles,
Tip-of-her-nose spectacles,

Her book on her crossed knees
The Poems of Dylan Thomas
Open at 'Fern Hill':

'Can one ever have too much of "Fern Hill"?
Swans, dons, students, secretaries going away from me
On stairs and corridors.

The most banal 2007 day is as much an apocalypse
In UCD as it was in Fern Hill
In Wales in the nineteen-twenties.'

Dorothy Molloy of Fern Hill, Mayo, Barcelona and UCD,
Dee-dum dee-dum-dee-doh
Fetching ten thousand dollars at a pinch,
I'm a – I'm a – I'm a Cubist in Cataluña
Going, going, gone –
And I always was and I always will be,
Gone,
Dah dee-dee-dee,
A Cubist in Cataluña, dah-dah dah-dee!

Portrait of the Painter as a Creature of Painstaking Courtesy

in memoriam Edward McGuire

My mother is sitting alone at my bedside.
A knock on the door. The door opening.

Chiaroscuro man in sunglasses and curls
Gripping, as 'twere the reins of a white horse,
The handle of a canvas shopping sack
Brimming with vegetables and fruit.

He visits for twenty minutes
Conversing with my mother
About vegetables and fruit –
Price vis-à-vis quality.
Leeks and avocados are what he vouches for
But my mother expostulates
She lacks experience of leeks and avocados.
I sit up in the bed, listening in consternation
To the pair of them, total strangers,
Being truly polite to one another.

He plunges his hand down into vegetables,
Fetches up a book wrapped in newspaper;
A small volume in red cloth and gold tooling,
The Discourses of Sir Joshua Reynolds;
On the flyleaf in flowing hand in black ink:

His name, address, telephone number.

'Paul, this is the book in which Reynolds —
Reynolds says it all.
It will help you to get well.
Return it to me when you're recovered.'

When he stands up to take his leave,
Holding out his hand to shake my mother's hand,
He bends down and kisses the back of her hand,
The small, fraught back of her hand.
She's not accustomed to the outrage of courtesy.
In the open door he glances back over his shoulder
And, employing the Italian form of farewell,
Pianissimo he pronounces it: *Salute.*

When the door closes behind him
My mother sits upright in her chair
And I lie back down in the bed
In silence. Plumbing humming.
She cries out: 'Who was that man?
I've never met a more courteous man in my life.'

On a cold spring day
I walk across Scotsman's Bay
To return to the most courteous man
My mother ever met in her life
The small volume in which Reynolds —
Reynolds says it all:
The great end of the art is to strike the imagination . . .
The spectator is only to feel the result in his bosom.

Meeting a Neighbour in
the GP's Waiting Room

This morning at 10 a.m. in the GP's waiting room
I meet Mark Hebblethwaite! My neighbour!
Although we have been neighbours for twenty-eight
    years
We have never had a conversation. That's normal
For Dublin, Ireland since the 1980s,
During and since the Celtic Tiger *Götterdämmerung*.

At 10 a.m. on a mid-October morning
The pair of us find ourselves
Sitting opposite one another
In the Doctor's empty waiting room
Waiting for our annual flu jab.
He is seventy-one. I am sixty-eight.

When he is called in first, he winks
'I'll wait for you.'
Here we are! Two old boys,
Looking like – and feeling like –
Two schoolboys on our first day at school
Making friends with one another.

After my flu jab the doctor runs
A quick precautionary cancer probe on me,

Which detains me an extra fifteen minutes.
But my neighbour – and new-found friend –
Is waiting for me as he said he would.
He has kept his word!

We stroll back down the road in sunlight
Under the sycamores, still green in mid-October,
And the chestnut trees' spotted golden leaves
Sodden underfoot after a night of downpours:
Two village elders risking freedom
In Orwell's Ireland of 2012.

At the awkward moment of parting –
Of SUNDERING, for good God's sake! –
Quite unexpectedly he inquires
'Would you like a cup of tea?'
As I procrastinate (if there was
An Olympic Gold Medal for Procrastination

I am the boy who would win it; I'd leave
Hamlet standing in the halfpenny place
In the Procrastination Stakes)
I am wondering if he means tea in the local café.
Sensing my dilemma, he elucidates: 'in *my* house'.
In *his* house? An unheard-of invitation,

Which I accept with alacrity. He murmurs
'You get your newspapers and I'll put the kettle on –
You know which abode I abide in – 33.'

His house fronts onto the street, its spiky ivy
    crimson,
Its masses of Virginia creeper golden red.
'This is a Victorian house,' he announces demurely

As he opens the door to me.
Every five minutes like a church bell
During our taking of the tea
He reiterates it: 'This is a Victorian house.'
It is an authentic Victorian house;
Himself an authentic Victorian Renaissance man;

A reticent, reserved, conscientious cavalier;
An urbane, gallant, erudite, sensualist;
A Pre-Raphaelite with iron in his soul.
We sit in the tiled and arched kitchen
Facing one another across an oak table
Naming mutual friends and favourite authors:

Harry Clifton, George Szirtes, Seamus Heaney,
Caitríona O'Reilly, James Plunkett, Maurice Keen,
Deirdre Madden, Wendy Cope, Eiléan Ní
    Chuilleanáin, Pier Paolo Pasolini.
The kettle has boiled and while the tea draws
He has time to change into short pants.
I blush with embarrassment. If only I had thought

To bring my own short pants with me, but at sixty-
    eight –

I was sixty-eight yesterday! –
One is inclined to leave one's short pants at home.
Incongruous as I am in my long pants
(Tediously corrugated brown corduroy trousers)
I do feel the frisson of being a boy again

On my first day at school,
Making friends with another new boy.
That he happens to be my neighbour of twenty-
    eight years
Is no longer here nor there
Or, rather, it is very, very, very much here.
Oh, if only I had brought with me my marbles!

Oh, if only I had brought with me my conkers!
Oh, if only I had brought with me my yo-yo!
Oh, if only I had a home of my own
I could invite him to come and look at my albums:
My stamp album, my autograph album, my
    photograph album!
As we part at his gate, keeping a straight bat,

He quotes Charles Tomlinson
With a twinkle in his eye. Charles Tomlinson!
On the beauty of that which is purely fortuitous –
The beauty of rhyme being like making friends.
Oh, for a few lines of friendship
If only once in a lifetime every twenty-eight years.

17 October 2012

The Talk in the GP's Waiting Room
Again and Again and

Three old ladies and, well, I suppose,
One old man (for is that not what I am? –
Come on, no more euphemism –
I am an old man naked in my shower
Toppling towards my denouement –
'Your DE-KNOT-MENT'
Lady in the corner barks at me).
The eighty-year-old lady opposite me
Pipes up on her squeaky didgeridoo:
'Am I imagining it this morning or is it really warm?'
We assure her in unison that she is not imagining it.
Despite the fine rain it is a really warm morning.
Old Lady in the Corner has buses on her mind:
'You'd be waiting an age for the 47.
An hour, at least. As for the 1 –
The 1 has gone to pot. Did you know
There is a play on in town called *Waiting for Godot*?
In the Gaiety Theatre. Did you ever hear of it?
It's a walking howl! The daughter-in-law
Brought me to it. No, no, no, no –
Not the TV series – the play! By a Foxrock man.
She told me his name, but now, of course,
Can I remember it? Not a fear of that.
The 47 leaves from Fleet Street on the hour

From outside The Oval pub.'

I interrupt her – circumspectly:

'I thought The Oval was in Abbey Street?'

Her two pinched, wizened chimp's eyes become two
cheeky schoolgirls:

'Ah yes, but you see – you have two Ovals!'

I stare at her in bewildered embarrassment.

She rubs her hands between her knees with glee.

'Oh yes, indeed, you have not one but two Ovals!'

I exclaim: 'That Foxrock man – was his name Beckett?'

'The VERY man!' she screams 'the VERY man!'

Sleepover

I was out pushing my Zimmer frame,
Estimating for the billionth time
I must be stark raving insane
To be eking it out in such a cold climate –
O what a bloody awful cold country we eke it out in! –
When she stopped me and said 'How are you?'
And I gurgled, 'I'm – I'm – I'm freezing to death!'
And we got chatting and sort of giggling
And I got so excited I nearly let go
Of the Zimmer and she shrieked
'How about a cup of tea?'
And when I shrieked back '*Mais oui!*'
She waved her stick in the air
And nearly lost her footing.
Then we had a bite in the Bistro
And then a drink in the House
On the corner and then two drinks
And then three drinks and then four drinks
And before you could say
'BLOW ME!'
She said, 'You're dead right!'
And she slept in my bed that night
And she slept in my bed the next night
And that was two winters ago
And she's still sleeping in my bed –
What the grandchilder call

'A sleepover' –
And she's still saying 'You're dead right!'
In fact, now she's saying
'You're *always* dead right!'
Oh, I never thought I'd live to see
My little fellow rise up again,
My wee Lazarus,
But rise up he did and she opened her arms wide
Like James Larkin *in excelsis*
And – do you know what she did? –
She clasped me!
She clasped and she clasped and she clasped and she
    clasped and she clasped me!
I was fit to die, I was!

Athy, County Kildare

'A side of Athy I'd never seen before,'
She sighed – and I laughed – and she laughed.
She'd always been a connoisseur of thigh
And the sides of thighs. We were ambling
Along the wide banks
Where the River Barrow meets the Grand Canal
And I had met Aimée MacDonald a year ago
At what looked like the end of our lives.
Yes – at the end of our lives! How accidental!
How dangerous! How heretical! How comical!
We ambled along, hand in hand, while she discoursed,
On the outskirts of Athy,
On the thigh and the sides of a thigh.
'To awake and open your eyes and see alongside you
An expanse of thigh – like a slice of Sahara:
Pure white sand, slightly mottled,
And to run your fingers along it and through it,
Caressing and stroking it,
Until suddenly it begins to shift and shudder
And a great nameless unknown obelisk
Erupts out of the desert sands
And you have no choice but to grapple
With it from plinth to eye,
And initially you scratch
A thigh gently as you can but finally
You are compelled to dig deep your fingernails into it

And the obelisk bays in delight and torment
With all its horns and all its bugles
And from out the sand as well as from the sky
Gushes unstoppable red-hot rain.'
'Oh, my God, no, yes!' I cry
In a side of Athy
'And, then, with great good luck, I do not die!'

For Brian Friel on His Eighty-Fifth Birthday

I

Thursday, 9 January 2014 –
Brian Friel's Eighty-fifth birthday –
Feast Day also of St Philip of Moscow,
Martyred by Tsar Ivan the Terrible –

I stood on the Rock of Dunamase,
Abashed to have known a saint-poet;
A saint-poet who is not a star,
But a sickle moon in a stream

In spate in the bottoms,
Gleaned through birch trees;
In a marshal's cast-off greatcoat
Buttoned up to the collar.

On the Rock of Dunamase,
Scanning the Central Plain
In the blue yellow day,
I cried out his name

To the Slieve Blooms and the Hill of Allen;
To Mountmellick and Mountrath and Ratheniska;
To Clonaslee and Rosenallis and Emo;
To the Great Heath of Maryborough.

A saint-poet who is not only a saint-poet
But a pure craftsman like a pure ceramicist:
A human kiln of compassion and anger;
Of laughter, of tears.

A man of grief, a man of joy;
A man of family, a man of friends;
A man averse to ballyhoo –
All that is journalistic and untrue.

The truth of Brian Friel's poetry is true.
Brian Friel has not perjured himself.
The truth of his poetry is as milky blue
As the black of the blackest sky.

II

Who is Brian Friel? Is he real?
Although a genius I have a feeling
He is real – I saw him with my own eyes
Riding a Vespa scooter across the bogs of Mayo
With a woman at his back, clinging to him
With a smile as big as Donegal on her face.

I had the brass neck to stop Brian Friel
And speak with him briefly – seven and a half
   minutes –
On the road between Bellacorick and Ballycroy.
He told me that he was en route to Belmullet
The real name of which was St Petersburg.
'Belmullet!' he cried. 'Belmullet is St Petersburg!

Oh, the lights of St Petersburg!
First glimpsed from the north shore of Achill!'
'Adieu!' I cried to him, clasping his hand in warm
  friendship.

III

St Philip of Moscow spent most of his life as a monk
In the monastery of Solovetsky, beside the White Sea;
Brian Friel has spent most of his life as a married
  monk
In a hermitage on Inishowen on the shores of Lough
  Foyle.

God rejects him who does not love his neighbour.
I have to tell you, though I die for it.

Mrs Denise Willa Vicky Charles
Murphy-O'Conor

No, I agree.
I would not be
The pathetic, miserable, catatonic skunk that I am
Had I one iota of the determination
Of the female house sparrow.
Look at her!
(Are you hearing me? I am complaining: Look at her!)

No matter the bare
Foliage of the forsythia,
The female house sparrow
Cares not a whit,
Flies through it – zoom! –
Day in, day out,
Midwinter,
Drear after drear day,
Low-level light that is not light,
Crashing into the sash window
Again and again
To perch on the cross-strut,
Nibble at flaking, off-white paintwork,
Peck at antique windowpane.

Eccentric? Indeed, doctor!
The female house sparrow is so irremediably eccentric
That there is none to compare with her.
Why, Maestro Death, let us be candid:
The female house sparrow sets your nerves on edge,
For you cannot match her
For her audacity, her integrity,
Her female omniscience,
Her private cheek,
Her sheer off-the-wall indifference
To what you or I think of her,
Her exuberance in her own refusal to conform
To your rules or anyone else's rules;
Her exuberance in the gaps in her knowledge;
She wears what she likes when she likes
Where she likes or nothing at all,
While you bestride your chamber pot,
Perusing gravely the broadsheets
Or *Hello!* magazine,
You pompous ninny!
She is out there in the street
Doing the messages:
Doing the business.
Unspeakable!
Female
House sparrow enigma!
We call her Denise –
Mrs Denise Willa Vicky Charles Murphy-O'Conor!

Earthquake Off Mayo

Yes –
I heard the earthquake.
Jumped out of bed.
Looked out the window –
Could see nothing.
Got back into bed.

6 June 2012

Beau Durcan

for Maud and Oscar and Beau and Florence and Jude

From a peninsular townland on the west coast of
    Ireland
I am the curator of a stammer so staggering
It makes Niagara Falls look like a lost rivulet
Of reticent water – flat, tranquil, silent, hidden,
Circumspect water from a spring well.
It is 1954, I am twelve years old.
My name is Beau – Beau Durcan –
And for that reason also I am the prey
Of the crew-cut bully-boys of my boarding school,
As well as of the more sadistic among the Jesuit priests
Who are my schoolmasters. I hate every stone and
    mullion
Of the castle in which the school is housed
In its affectation of being the Eton of Ireland,
And I can survive only by grace of benefit of my dream
Of my family home in the west – of my beautiful
    mother, my gay sisters,
My baby brother,
By the black-and-amber seaweed on the shores of
    Rosbeg.
Not even I can tell you what it is like
To be the curator of a monumental stammer
At the age of twelve years,

No more than a boy born without fingers
Can tell you what it is like to be fingerless.
To me a single vocable of the English language
Is a tornado approaching from the horizon –
The horizon being the pit of my stomach.
A word beginning with the consonant 'b'
Thickens, darkens, dilates, billows, knocks me down
And a bean-pole, self-important male of the species
In a pin-stripe suit with pin-stripe wings and pin-stripe
    biretta
Looks down at me, laughing at me,
And mocks me. '*Baile?* Home?
Is that what you are cavorting to utter? *Baile?* Home?
Well, listen here to me, young Beau,
There is no such thing as home –
No such place. There is only equity.
Do you hear me? Stop stammering about home.
Moreover, my little man,
Stop permitting your mother and sisters to call you
    "Beau".
Beau is a feminine, French word, inappropriate for a
    boy's name,
Not to mention heathenish, suggestive, secular.'

And so I grew up in fear and trembling
.That not even Søren Kierkegaard could have fathomed,
But I took advantage of being a little fellow
And by fifteen I had cultivated all the knacks of the
    craft

Of the professional jockeys on the tracks of England
 and Ireland,
Assiduously reading the racing pages, studying the
 form,
How to squeeze through the middle, how to come on
 the inside,
How to transfer my whip from left hand to right,
 sparingly,
Lore I would pass on to my own son,
Our champion Ted.

The King Bullies of Clongowes Wood College
Are all long dead and gone,
But I am still stammering like an angel
Long able to smile in Purgatory
And on through the Gates of Paradise.
The gentleness of God is beyond all telling –
For God also has a stammer of purest gold:
How otherwise did He create the world,
The cosmos, the universe, the sun, moon and stars
Except by stammering it all into existence and being?
Listen to me: I am Beau Durcan;
I speak the language of sea water and rowlocks;
Ship oars with me now.

3 February 2014

Shaking Hands with Seán Ralph in the Middle of the Street at the Intersection of Sandymount Green and Claremont Road

Every time I set eyes on Seán Ralph –
He whose grandmother Mary Byrne in 1879
Witnessed the Apparition of the Mother of God
At Knock, County Mayo, on a wet August night –
I go leaping across the street to shake his hand.
Seán Ralph is eighty-four years old, if a day,
Trimmer and gayer and more debonair
And more full of bounce and news and extraordinary
    courtesy
Than any other living male human being in Sandymount,
Ringsend, Irishtown – the Three Villages –
And always he has just come back from somewhere!

I say to him: 'I can see by the glint in your eye
Under that mickey dazzler flat white cap of yours
That you've just come back from somewhere – from
    where?'
Surreptitiously he issues a smile, enamelled with
    excitement:
'Chicago,' he whispers. 'Where?' 'Chicago!
Chicago for a month! It was my daughter Eileen's fiftieth.

God Almighty, Paul, we had a great old time of it.
There's nowhere in the world to beat Chicago,
    nowhere.'

Nevertheless, while not able to top that,
I am able to tell him that during the summer
I visited a schoolteacher, Noel Rowland, near Manulla –
Manulla, County Mayo – Seán Ralph's home place,
From where he emigrated fifty or sixty years ago.
I tell him how the schoolteacher pointed out to me
The original post office run by the Ralph family.
Mr Seán Ralph, aged eighty-four years, of Sandymount
    and Chicago,
Draws himself up to his full, erect height
Of nearly six feet, bursting out laughing: 'That was
    OUR house!'
'YOUR house?' 'OUR house!'
'On the corner of the crossroads
Where the roads to Balla and Ballyvary meet?'
'OUR house!'
'God, Seán – it's a bloody dangerous corner!'
'Paul, you can say that again and
Do you know something else, Paul?
In the 1950s I used to cycle over the hills to Turlough
    village,
Where your people the Durcans had the pub –
I used to cycle over for the dance in Turlough dance
    hall
And, do you know what? Fifty years later in Chicago
One of your Turlough boys said to me:

"You're an awful man, Seán Ralph,
Cycling over the hills from Manulla to Turlough
To steal our girls! In point of actual fact,
You almost stole our most beautiful girl, Mary Conway!"
And, do you know something else, Paul?
It's always a pleasure to meet you. Have a nice day,
    Paul.'
'God bless you, Seán.'
By now we have established a foothold on the far
    footpath:
Smiling or glaring motorists having circled around us
For the six or seven minutes of our *conversazione*.
Before walking off separately in opposite directions –
For the third time, formally, we shake hands.

2 October 2013

Death of a Mason –
Brave Brian Sheridan

Brian Sheridan wasn't twenty-four hours in his
   Protestant grave
In St Thomas' Churchyard in Dugort,
Diligently dug by his Catholic neighbours
Drowning in the Acacia spray,
Between his Russian mother and his Irish father,
But he was out of it and up at my six-barred gate –
Black face, white hair –
On the lower slopes of the mountain,
Where sheep may safely graze,
Reclining in the quartz in the mud under my gate
Licking himself – *infernal midges!* –
Old ram chewing away, brandishing his horns
At all the other fleeces – wethers, ewes, hoggets,
   lambs –
He had awoken from their grave-slumber:
Vi, Arthur, Cyril, Rebecca, Girly, Harold, June, Gladys.
If there was one thing you could say for Brian
   Sheridan,
He was an Old Believer in the Resurrection.

27 June 2013

In Memoriam: The Guinea

He was christened Patrick John Gallagher
But from the days of his childhood
He was never known by any name
Other than 'The Guinea'.
The day after The Guinea's funeral –
He died of cancer aged seventy-five years –
I went back up to the tall, thin graveyard –
A black eyepatch of a graveyard on a bare hillside
In Bunacurry looking down on the sea.
It was empty, of course, just me and a lark
Or two and the breeze and bits of sunlight.
I sat on the kerb of somebody else's grave
Near The Guinea, chatting to him:
'What's it like down there
In that six-foot hole in the ground?
I couldn't sleep for thinking of you
In the long rain we had last night –
You vast-hearted, tender-necked rascal.'
Suddenly I stood up and started to shout:
'GOODBYE PATRICK JOHN – GOODBYE
    MICHAEL MARTIN –
GOODBYE TEDDY LAVELLE! GOODBYE!'
I walked quickly up and down the graveyard,
Carefree and vigorous and punching the air:
'GOODBYE! GOODBYE! GOODBYE! GOODBYE!'
I stalked out the gate, not closing it behind me.

Getting into my car
I spotted The Guinea in the clouds above me –
At least a mile up above the white horses of the sea –
Smiling down upon me – like he always used to do –
His saintly, piratical smile –
Never was there nothing
That The Guinea would not do for you –
I waved up to him out of my driving-seat window:
'Who is that laughing fisherman?'
I cried. 'Who is he?'
'Sure, isn't it me?' cried The Guinea.
'Wasn't I always the sun, moon and stars?
Goodbye to you too. I'll be seeing you!'

17 August 2013

The Navigator
after Veronica Bolay

Sick to death of poets and bogs I flew –
I flew from Ireland to New Zealand.

Dublin, Gatwick, Colorado, Hawaii,
Auckland, Wellington:
In a field in the hills overlooking Wellington
A little girl ran up to me crying out
'Look, I found a pebble!'

In the next field stood a small, frame house
Of timber walls and timber doors painted blue
With hieroglyphics of a life I had not known
And but for now might never get to know:
'Look, I found a pebble!'

She kept on running towards me – running past me –
Her full lips convulsed, blurred
In her flying red skirt and her flying white shirt –
Crying out until she had disappeared out of sight:
'Look, I found a pebble!'

2 July 2014

Kitty of Portlaoise

in memoriam Kitty Stapleton O'Neill (1913–2014)

Hit base-camp dejection this morning and knew –
Having been guided with charity, patience, humour
And all the labours of affection by a Sherpa goddess –
I would have to shove off – find some other virgin
  mountain
In which to bury my head and subsist alone
And eventually, inevitably, return the gift of life.

Mid-afternoon – having hauled myself out of my
  sleeping bag –
I stood at the window staring at the tour-de-force
  performance
Of the choral forces of snowdrops
Inside the low box hedge under the cherry tree:
Their choreography – as always
And in spite of my excruciating despondency –
Astonished me! Across the stage from left to right
Flocks of snowdrops in threes and fours, sevens and
  eights –
In numbers adding up to hundreds –
Purity of innocence that can never be a prey to
  cynicism,
Never scorned, never regretted, never presumed, never
  rationalised.

When *enduring* – it's always by dint of *enduring* –
The gazing melted from my staring:
The binoculars of fading eyesight focussed abruptly
And I saw among these hundreds of snowdrops
A few feet away from me beneath the windowsill
Three large brown rats snouting about in the clay of the
    sparse grass –
In the twigs and the roots and the seeds fallen from
    bird-feeders.
My first instinct was to flit in flitters –
Flit, flit, flit, flit, flit! –
To flit in flitters as far as I could –
Get into the car – my grim little technical-grey
    Opel Astra – and drive –
Drive anywhere. Disappear like the disorientated
    asylum-seeker that I am.

I compelled myself, coiling my own arms, to stand and
    watch
The three rats burrowing among the snowdrops,
And within less than ten minutes I came to recognise –
    appreciate even –
Their concentration on what they were doing; their
    prop-forward
Concentration, their scholarly attention to minutiae,
A triad of goggle-eyed history professors poring over the
    archives of the dead.
Oh, how self-contained they were! How self-satisfied!
    How well-fed!
Beside and behind them picked

A single robin redbreast and a single blackbird,
Neither of whom took the blindest bit of notice
Of the three rats nor the three rats of them:
Above the rats on a bare bough of cherry
A blue tit considered its options.

'Rats – what pleasant company rats can be
I discovered all alone in my bare prison cell!'
My Russian grand-aunt whispered to me
On her deathbed in Ratoath near Fairyhouse,
Her wet eyes scooped open, gleaming, dreaming, smiling:
'Rats – what pleasant company rats can be!'
All alone on her deathbed, the most glamorous – but
    for Kitty – old lady of all.

The low-level, winter-westering sun lit up the stage
And I knew that once-off audience-sensation
That I was a privileged spectator –
That although I died a death this morning
(Attended my own funeral and burial –
Crouched alone at my own obsequies)
In actuality the only significant event of this day
Had been the presentation by the snowdrops,
By the blackbird, the robin, the blue tit
And the three large brown rats, all hump and tail,
And I heard my beloved Kitty of Portlaoise admonish
    me sternly:
'Get a life.'

13 February 2014